More Praise for
Against the Grain

"Joel Stern has built a renowned business based on strong intellectual ideas. Joel describes how he did it, with characteristic openness and great humor. It is an excellent read."

> Julian Franks
> Professor
> London Business School

"*Against the Grain* opens the door gently to the mysteries of corporate finance but then casts a sharp and critical view over established practice. The question of assessing the underlying health and prospects for companies, now so topical after the bursting of the share-price bubble, is addressed with intellectual vigor . . . mixed with the human side of business as Joel Stern describes his own life story and the many personalities who have influenced him."

> Charles Jenkins
> Director, Western Europe
> *Economist* Intelligence Unit

"One of the many good deeds done by the wholly admirable Harry Oppenheimer (late Chairman of South Africa's leading companies, Anglo-American and De Beers), was to introduce the country's business leaders, academics, and students to Joel Stern, who has informed, instructed, and inspired them. He has brought us his unique brand of deep financial insight and his passion for much improved financial management, all this combined with a wonderful wit that makes every interaction with him not only useful but entertaining."

> Brian Kantor
> Professor of Economics
> University of Cape Town

Against the Grain

Against the Grain

How to Succeed in Business by Peddling Heresy

Joel M. Stern
with Irwin Ross

WILEY

John Wiley & Sons, Inc.

Published by John Wiley & Sons, Inc., Hoboken, New Jersey.
Published simultaneously in Canada.

For general information on our other products and services, or technical support, please contact our Customer Care Department within the United States at 800-762-2974, outside the United States at 317-572-3993 or fax 317-572-4002.

Wiley also publishes its books in a variety of electronic formats. Some content that appears in print may not be available in electronic books.

For more information about Wiley products, visit our web site at www.wiley.com.

Library of Congress Cataloging-in-Publication Data:

Stern, Joel M.
  Against the grain : how to succeed in business by peddling heresy /
Joel M. Stern with Irwin Ross.
    p. cm.
  ISBN 0-471-21600-3 (cloth)
  1. Economic value added. 2. Corporations—Valuation. 3. Capital
investments—Decision making. 4. Managerial economics. I. Ross, Irwin.
II. Title.
  HG4028.V3S828 2003
  338.6'041'092—dc21

                        2003010884

Printed in the United States of America.

10 9 8 7 6 5 4 3 2 1

To my son, Erik Daniel, who has shown us the real meaning of beautiful feelings on the inside accompanied by a desire to innovate and inspire us. This is leadership in all of its aspects.

Contents

Photographs appear after page 110.

Foreword

John S. Shiely

If the Royal Swedish Academy of Sciences awarded prizes for groundbreaking advances in applied microeconomics (and by all rights they should), Joel Stern should have received one years ago.

Equally adept at operating in the spheres of both academia and business, Joel Stern has made an unparalleled contribution in converting economic theory into microeconomic tools of practical application that go to the heart of creating value in the firm. In coining the now widely used terms "free cash flow" and "lead steers" and in promoting the twin heresies of "Earnings per share don't count" and "Dividends don't matter," Joel swam against a strong current of conventional financial dogma. He views himself as a missionary. "Evangelist" might be a more appropriate term. He is the "Albert Schweitzer of shareholder value."

Joel's pedigree is extraordinary. With teachers of the ilk of Merton Miller, Milton Friedman, Harry Johnson, and George Stigler and with classmates on the order of Myron Scholes, Michael Jensen, and Richard Roll, he experienced firsthand the golden age of Chicago School economic thought. It should not be surprising that he was viewed as a radical in the circles of conventional financial practice.

He has been a catalyst for change—radical change in financial concepts of strategy and incentive systems intended to mold behavior in the firm. When the roots of your beliefs are in economic theory, it is very easy for the hardened financial practitioners to write you off as one who operates outside the "real world." The burden of proof that your beliefs are confirmed by actual market performance no doubt seems insurmountable. It is ironic that the most important contribution Joel Stern has made is in converting controversial economic theory into readily available practical applications that can be understood by people who have not been trained in finance and accounting. Small wonder that there are now folks on the shop floor who understand the process of value creation better than the deans at some prestigious business schools.

His career achievements have been impressive. He headed up the Chase Manhattan Financial Policy group at a very young age and founded and nurtured Stern Stewart, one of the most successful financial consulting firms in the world. He has been a frequent contributor to the editorial pages of the *Wall Street Journal* and the *Financial Times*, and was a 17-year regular panelist on Louis Rukeyser's *Wall Street Week*. His academic credentials are equally impressive, having served on the faculty at, among others, the Columbia University Graduate School of Business; the Carnegie Mellon University Graduate School of Industrial Administration; the Simon School at the University of Rochester; the University of Witswatersrand and the University of Cape Town, both in South Africa; the University of Michigan; and the London Business School.

Joel Stern is probably best known for his collaboration with Bennett Stewart in the development of the discipline of EVA (Economic Value Added), which regression analysis has clearly shown is the best available method of enhancing shareholder value. The key concepts of EVA practice are that cash is king (accounting results need to be restated to reflect economic reality) and that capital—both debt and equity—has a cost and must be deployed efficiently. These might seem to be simple concepts, but the process of value creation faces some very significant hurdles in practice: the distributive tendencies of politicians and trade unions, regulatory regimes hostile toward value creation, and entrenched management oblivious to agency issues, not to mention the antiquated financial perceptions of some capital providers. The EVA discipline rigorously rejects the, by now, well-publicized distortions of accounting practice. It would not be an overstatement to observe that if Enron, WorldCom, and Tyco had committed to the EVA discipline, their destinies would have been very different.

But this book is about more than Joel Stern's achievements in shaping economic thought and financial practices. It is about the life challenges of an incredibly driven individual. I must admit to a strong bias here, as I count Joel among my closest friends.

EVA was a key element of our turnaround program at Briggs & Stratton in the late 1980s. In fiscal 1989, we reported the first financial loss in our company's history since our listing on the New York Stock Exchange in 1929. Like many rust-belt metal benders, we had overinvested in automation initiatives in an attempt to improve productivity in an intensely high cost operating environment in our main plant in Milwaukee. We had been sucked into the labor/capital trade-off vortex in which cost improvements are claimed when the economic gain achieved represents only a modest improvement. When we adopted EVA as our primary performance metric and applied it to our incentive programs, strategic planning, organizational design, and corporate development initiatives, the results were impressive. We rather rapidly began an unbroken streak of nine years of positive EVA.

EVA is more than an economic discipline; it is a behavioral discipline. And superior EVA performance is achieved through more integrative relationships with various corporate constituencies. Yes, we'll give the line workers more compensation, but they'll have to work with us to increase productivity. Yes, we'll give the customers price reductions, but they'll have to work with us to engineer costs and capital out of the total product and process. And as these high-value relationships are developed, new solutions are engineered that are much less capital intensive and more capital efficient. That is how we worked our way out of the labor/capital trade-off vortex at Briggs & Stratton, and many other companies have adopted the EVA discipline with similar success.

Our EVA implementation program at Briggs & Stratton was headed by Joel's partner, Bennett Stewart. Although I had met Joel and had had the opportunity to discuss various issues with him, it was not until I was asked to address the management team at the U.S. Postal Service on the implementation challenges of EVA that I had the chance to work directly with Joel on one of his projects. This led to a number of "tag team" seminars, in which Joel described the EVA regimen and I addressed implementation issues. The most notable of these events were our presentations to the *Fortune* 500 CEO Forum in San Francisco and the World Economic Development Congress in Washington, D.C. (at the latter event, we were the "opening act" for Henry Kissinger). A Joel Stern presentation has all the intensity of a tent revival and the intellectual content of a *Harvard Business Review* article. It has been a pleasure playing Joel's sidekick in spreading the word.

Joel's vocation is financial consulting; his avocation is baseball. My vocation is corporate management; and my avocation is performing rock 'n' roll music. Joel has introduced me (literally) to such leading economists (some laureates) as Merton Miller, Myron Scholes, Gary Becker, Michael Jensen and Peter Drucker (a huge advocate of EVA). I have introduced him (literally) to rock 'n' roll icons Ray Charles, the Beach Boys, and Buddy Holly's Crickets. I've probably gotten the better of these exchanges, but I think we both would admit that we are better off for these left brain/right brain transplants.

Joel has aptly titled his work *Against the Grain: How to Succeed in Business by Peddling Heresy*; and he has retained Irwin Ross, one of the finest business writers in the profession, to assist him in the effort. It is not only a worthy read for anyone interested in the development of the theories and practice of value creation, but also a fascinating account of one man's struggle to sell a concept in which he believes passionately.

Against the Grain

1

The Great Break

July 27, 1982, was the day that changed my life, at least my business life. That morning, after weeks of deliberation, I walked into my boss's office and resigned from the Chase Manhattan Bank, where I headed a group called Chase Financial Policy, a corporate finance advisory service for the bank's customers. After 18 years at the bank, resigning was not easy; and when I returned to my office I had that slightly giddy sense of triumph that comes from taking a long-delayed, decisive step. As I walked through the door, my secretary, Pauline Yavel, quickly brought me back to earth. "Your 9:30 appointment is here," she said. The visitor was Ron Palamara of Anacomp, an Indiana company that specialized in software for banks.

"What can I do for you, Ron?" I asked.

"I have another assignment for you," he announced, whereupon I told him that I had resigned and was going to start my own business. As I outlined my plans, the thought crossed my mind that Palamara might be interested in backing me. Anacomp had a reputation for paying too much for acquisitions and maybe it would do so again. But I made no pitch, for Palamara was soon asking, "What is your business worth?"

"Ten million dollars," I replied instantly. I had made no calculation. Ten million sounded like a nice round number. And it was plausible.

"Would $5 million buy half the company?" Palamara asked. I said, "It sure would." Ron picked up the phone and dictated a letter of intent to his secretary in Indianapolis. We got the money— $2 million in cash, the rest in Anacomp shares—late in October. On November 1, 1982, Stern Stewart & Co. (originally called Stern Stewart Putnam & Macklis) opened for business in a modest office in midtown Manhattan. The staff consisted of nine partners and one secretary.

Out of that humble beginning we built a global financial consulting firm, headquartered in New York, with other offices in Los Angeles, London, Munich, Mumbai (formerly Bombay), Bangkok, Johannesburg, Melbourne, Sao Paulo, Singapore, Beijing, Shanghai, and Tokyo. Over the years, our clients have constituted a roster of the great and near-great corporate names—from Coca-Cola to Siemens AG to Quaker Oats to Mexico's Vitro and Pemex; from Herman Miller to Millenium Chemicals to SPX; from the U.S. Postal Service to Telecom New Zealand; from Banc One to the ABSA bank of South Africa; from Best Buy to JC Penney and Toys R Us to Metro in Germany, the JD Group and New Clicks in South Africa, and Tata and Godrej in India.

What did we do for them? In the flattering phrase that one admirer applied to us, our firm has been a "catalyst for change." I am happy to embrace the phrase, for basically we have been selling our clients change—fundamental change, radical change—in financial concepts, strategy, and incentive systems that involve abandoning long-established doctrines and practices. From the outset, we crusaded against the shibboleths and distortions of accounting practices, focusing instead on the underlying economic reality of the firm. To that end, we developed the concept of Economic Value Added (EVA), which is both a measurement tool and a total

2

management system, including an incentive plan. We marketed it with great success as the best available method of enhancing shareholder value, a goal much touted in recent years but one often neglected in practice.

EVA is a proprietary system, which we have installed in more than 300 companies worldwide. But so much has been written about EVA, by myself and others (notably by my partner Bennett Stewart, who published the first book on the subject), that it has also become a generic concept. We have competitors who have been selling their own versions of EVA, and some companies have attempted to install the program on their own. Naturally, we push our own system, but becoming generic has to be taken as a large token of success.

But to go back to the beginning of the tale that culminated in 1982. For more than a dozen years at Chase Manhattan, I had been successfully peddling change in the way that firms handled financial strategy. To those bank clients who would listen to me, I advocated decidedly nontraditional approaches to valuation, dividend policy, capital structure, acquisitions, and divestitures (but not EVA, which had not yet been invented). At the time, my views were considered downright heretical, though they were based on sound academic research largely generated by scholars at or from the University of Chicago. The tone of my heresy was typified by two slogans I popularized: "Earnings-per-Share Doesn't Count" and "Dividends Don't Matter." What did count was *free cash flow*—the cash that a company has in excess of all current cash requirements, including all planned new investment (a subject that I will later explore at some length). I saw myself as something of a missionary. I regarded it as my job to convert the heathen to the new doctrines coming out of Chicago. I was in my late twenties, young and brash and not above ridiculing the old wisdom.

Though most of the brass at the bank either did not understand or scorned my views, I had some followers among loan officers, with whom I used to call on clients. I had a considerable measure of success and enjoyed the freedom of running my own operation with a small staff of professionals, most of whom I had hired right out of graduate school. But I had learned enough about the art of survival in a large bureaucracy to know when the glory days were over. That realization suddenly hit me one day in February 1982 after I was summoned to Bob Lichten's office. He had been deputy to the bank's chief financial officer and was now second in command of the new investment bank that Chase was setting up. Lichten, a most affable man, told me that he and his boss wanted my unit, Chase Financial Policy, to be part of the new investment bank.

"But Bob, what does this mean?" I asked.

"It means that you will be in charge of the finance advisory function for the investment bank," he replied.

But I persisted. I wanted to know whether I would still be calling on clients or would be sequestered with my crew in some back office, crunching numbers. Specifically, who would be making presentations to the clients? Lichten conceded that the new bank's top people would handle the presentations. Apparently I looked distinctly unhappy, for Lichten then asked, "Don't you want to be a team player?" to which I riposted, "I am a team player, but I want to give independent advice."

Lichten then spoke graciously about how the bank valued my intellectual contributions over the years. But soft words could not appease me. I felt a rising flush of anger that I made no effort to repress and said—I can still remember the words—"Bob, if you think so highly of my advice, how come that in the five years that you have been in your job you never asked my opinion on anything?" I had to restrain myself from saying more.

Lichten's face stiffened. He said nothing. But I knew the game was up. Nonetheless, I called on James Carey, the head of the bank's domestic commercial loan operations, to whom I reported. I reminded Carey that in the past he had said that he would protect me. Carey felt compelled to correct me: "I said I'd protect you as long as

I could." Now he was powerless; top management wanted my unit to be in the investment bank and there was nothing he could do about it. He advised me to go along with the inevitable. I thanked him.

I knew I had no future at Chase, but I was not impetuous enough to resign on the spot. Instead, I went back to my group's offices in the Chase headquarters building and first told Bennett Stewart and then the other staff members what had happened and that I was thinking of leaving to start my own firm. Bennett, whom I had hired just after he got his MBA from Chicago six years before and who served as my deputy, immediately said that he would join me. So did most of the others. There was great esprit de corps in our group, a consequence of our relative autonomy and the sense that we were pioneers, selling what we regarded as a unique product. And the group was also relatively young, most being in their late twenties or early thirties (at 41, I was the oldest)—just the age to be able to afford entrepreneurial risk.

I was in no rush, however. Before I set up my own shop, I had to be assured that I would have clients, and I did what disaffected executives in my position always do—I canvassed my current clients. Discreetly, of course. As I visited them around the country and abroad, I would mention that I was thinking of setting up my own shop and hoped that I would retain their patronage. I specifically remember approaching Charles Knight of Emerson Electric, Ben Heineman of Northwest Industries, and Dr. Anton Rupert of the Rembrandt Group in South Africa. I got favorable responses from all of them. Rupert's encouragement was critical because of his eminence in the Afrikaner business community.

Then, to my vast embarrassment, word of my soundings got back to James Carey in New York. I was in Cape Town, South Africa, when I got a telex message from Carey ordering me home immediately. I phoned his secretary to plead for a delay, pointing out that I was giving a series of lectures at the University of Cape Town that would end in two weeks. But Carey was adamant that I return immediately. I made my apologies to the university rector, explaining that an emergency had come up, and flew back to New York. So, before 9 A.M. on July 27, I found myself in Carey's office. He was a brawny man, as solidly built as a football lineman, and he was absolutely livid. After dressing me down—"How could you be so stupid?"—he then asked, "Now what are you going to do about it?" I resigned on the spot.

Until that meeting with Carey, I must confess that I had a measure of ambivalence about leaving Chase. On the one hand, I had been quite successful at the bank and had enough admirers up the bureaucratic chain of command to flourish. I had, after all, been elected a vice president in 1970, when I was 29, which was regarded as a tender age for the job. I also enjoyed the cachet of representing Chase, then known as the Rockefeller bank. The Chase imprimatur seemed to validate ideas that might otherwise be dismissed as wildly impractical.

On the other hand, there was a downside in working for a large institution in a highly regulated industry, which to me always meant "protected" from entrepreneurial competitors, such as Goldman Sachs. Chase, like most commercial banks at the time, was not very entrepreneurial. It prized size and growth and institutional durability over economic profit; "shareholder value" was a term never heard. Individuals on an ascendant career path tended to avoid risk, for successful risk taking brought few rewards by way of incentive pay, and failure could mean the door. As at most banks, variable pay was a low proportion of total compensation. Moreover, apart from a few kindred souls outside my group who shared my interests, the atmosphere was amiable but intellectually dismal. Going it alone with a young hungry crew was hazardous but exciting.

The first office of our new company was in a Lexington Avenue suite of the Midland Bank of the United Kingdom. We enjoyed free rent, in return for which Midland put its name on our scholarly journal, which was edited by partner Don Chew. It had been the *Chase*

Financial Quarterly and was now the *Midland Corporate Financial Journal.* And within two years, we did well enough to buy back the 50 percent of the firm from Ron Palamara. Ten years later, most of the partners who stayed with the firm were millionaires, a commitment (or at least a promise) that I had made to each one who joined me on Day One.

2

Beginnings

This book is a business memoir, but I gather that a few personal details are mandatory. While I regard myself as the intellectual offspring of the University of Chicago—particularly of my teachers Milton Friedman and Merton Miller—my corporeal launch was more humble.

I was born in New York City on August 16, 1941, during a turbulent period in history—the second year of the Second World War, two months after Hitler invaded the Soviet Union and four months before the attack on Pearl Harbor, cataclysmic events that preoccupied my young parents but fortunately did not interfere with family formation. I was the second son born to Boris and Irene Stern, my brother, Russell, having preceded me by three years. Two sisters, Roberta and Jacqueline, followed my arrival within a few years.

Ours was a close-knit middle-class family, typical of many in New York then and now, scrupulously observant of orthodox Jewish ritual, passionately Zionist, and very liberal in domestic politics—the latter a great surprise to my friends in adult life, who assumed that I had been mouthing the maxims of Friedrich von Hayek since kindergarten. In our home, Franklin Delano Roosevelt was the secular deity, and the secular bible was the uninhibitedly liberal *New*

York Post, which only went to the right after Rupert Murdoch bought it in 1976.

My father was a strong personality whose standards of piety, compassion, and charity provided a model that I have always sought to emulate. If I had any latent rebellious instincts, they emerged in the political realm. But that came much later. My mother was a gentle person and a woman of exquisite esthetic sensibility who was especially gifted in the arts of home decoration. Whatever esthetic sense I possess I probably owe to her.

My parents were married for 64 years; both lived full and productive lives and died after protracted illnesses within nine months of each other in 2002. Their deaths were hard blows to sustain, no less poignant because they had long been foreshadowed—my mother had been hospitalized nine times within her last year, my father just once. Their children's pain was all the more acute because we had always seen a lot of each other. My New York City apartment has for years been within a mile of my parents, as was Roberta's home. Jacqueline lived nearby in Westchester County. Family dinners were frequent throughout the year. At Passover, the whole brood, spouses and children included, spent the entire week at a Westchester hotel. It was a cherished family retreat.

My grammar and high school years were spent at the Yeshiva Rabeinu Chaim Ozer, one of the many Jewish parochial schools in New York City. Our mornings were occupied with religious studies, the afternoons with secular subjects—science, math, social studies, English, the typical college-preparatory track. The school's aim was to instill a knowledge of Jewish law, tradition and ritual, as well as to teach us how to study and excel in the areas required for mundane success. Academic achievement was prized, with gold medals bestowed on A students and blue medals on B students. Most of us were highly competitive and I must confess to a degree of intellectual snobbishness—my friends were all gold medalists. Another strong memory of my school days was the central role played by charity.

Ever present in the school room, as at home, was the *pushkeh*—the cardboard collection box with a slitted metal top into which one regularly inserted coins for the charitable organization whose name was imprinted on the box.

Between home and school, I emerged with a profound sense of Jewish identity. And over the years I found no difficulty in combining traditional observances with upward mobility in the business world. I remember that in 1964, a few months after Barry Sullivan hired me to work at the Chase Manhattan Bank, I realized, as the autumn days grew shorter, that my Friday workday would not end before the arrival of the sabbath at sundown. There was no solution but for me to leave work early. I explained the situation to Barry, who was very understanding, perhaps because he was a devout Catholic. Then I had the impression that he thought I was asking for a one-time dispensation to leave early. I explained that the problem would recur every Friday until the spring, when the sun again set later. To reassure him, I suggested he talk to Rabbi Maurice Schwartz, the rabbi at our synagogue. Barry called the rabbi, who enlightened him on the theological niceties, and I was given carte blanche.

At home, of course, the Jewish dietary laws prevailed. But when eating out I "solved" the problem by not eating meat in non-kosher restaurants. Most of my associates are not aware that my passion for Dover sole meuniere in the French restaurants that we occasionally patronize is not solely a gastronomic preference.

In a city like New York, of course, there is an abundance of excellent kosher restaurants, but there can be a problem when traveling—not on airlines, all of which provide kosher meals (the kosher caterer on British Airways is particularly good). But kosher restaurants can be found in unexpected places. Not long ago, I was in Istanbul talking with a client who, it suddenly occurred to me, might be Jewish. I asked how long his people had been in Turkey. "Since 1492," he replied, explaining that after the Jews were expelled from Spain, his family fled east rather than south to Africa. We talked further about the ancient Jewish colony in Istanbul, and I finally asked him whether there was a kosher restaurant in town. Indeed there was, an elegant establishment, with but 14 tables, that was subsidized by a group of affluent Jewish businessmen. We went there the following night and were presented with a dazzling display of Turkish delicacies as well as traditional Jewish dishes, which originated in Eastern Europe. I felt quite at home.

But I am getting ahead of the tale. As a youngster, I had a passionate interest in baseball. I played a lot and at times entertained the fantasy of becoming a professional, but my enthusiasm was far greater than my talent. Like many of my friends, I was a Yankee fan and an avid collector of baseball cards. We all tried to swing a bat like Mickey Mantle; but unlike Mantle, who was a switch hitter, I could only bat right-handed. This was odd, because I was otherwise left-handed when I threw a ball or wrote. As for intellectual matters, when I grew a bit older, the youngster did not prefigure the adult. In both high school and college, I was absorbed by physics and math and had no interest in the social sciences or politics. As I look back, I have to conclude that I was a very dull fellow.

In September 1958, I entered the freshman class at the City College of New York, just after my seventeenth birthday. CCNY still enjoyed a reputation for academic excellence that has been justly celebrated in memoirs of the 1930s. The advent of open admissions, which led to a decline in standards, was still a few years away. Loading my schedule with math and physics courses, I managed not to take a single course in history or social science. I also managed to work out a combined program of graduate physics courses at Columbia University and undergraduate work at CCNY. I had met a professor named Harold Stolov, who taught at both institutions. Stolov's graduate courses at Columbia were more interesting than those he offered at CCNY and the authorities indulged me. It was my first selling job.

Stolov was of invaluable help to me in an odd way. He somehow discovered that I was not very attentive in class. I had difficulty concentrating; my mind worked quickly, but it would wander. I must have flubbed a few questions when he called on me amidst my reveries. But the professor did not humiliate me in front of my classmates; instead, he privately counselled me to discipline my vagrant thoughts, to learn to concentrate. I took his advice to heart and ultimately became a better student.

A short while prior to graduation from college in 1962, I had what can accurately be called an epiphany. As mentioned earlier, in politics my family was unrelentingly liberal. Around our table, the columnists in the *New York Post*—Murray Kempton, Max Lerner, James A. Wechsler—were attentively read and copiously quoted. The liberal worldview, which accorded a large and even a dominant role to government in ordering the affairs of men and institutions, was the only view to which I was exposed and one that I accepted unhesitatingly. Indeed, it never occurred to me that there was any other way of looking at the world.

Then, a few months before graduation, I read a short book by Milton Friedman called *Capitalism and Freedom*. A college friend, who had preceded me to the University of Chicago Graduate School of Business, sent me the book—actually not the book but a mimeograph copy of the manuscript, which had started life as a series of lectures. Reading those pages changed my life. For one thing, it led me to enroll at Chicago's Graduate School of Business.

To my innocent eyes, the book was a revelation. Friedman revived the nineteenth-century definition of a liberal (a term he applied to himself) as a person who believed in the widest measure of freedom in personal affairs and laissez faire in economic matters. He argued persuasively that personal freedom was dependent on the existence of free markets—on competitive capitalism. "So long as effective freedom of exchange is maintained," Friedman wrote, "the central feature of the market organization of economic activity is that it prevents one person from interfering with another in respect of most of his activities." He feared that in the ultimate collectivist society, where the government ran the economy and employed the labor force, the basic freedoms of speech and of assembly would wither because individuals would lack the job security to question the state.

One fascinating illustration of Friedman's thesis was his passage about the Hollywood blacklist in the 1950s, which denied employment to actors, writers, and directors suspected of Communist involvement. Friedman believed that anyone had a right not to associate with anyone else; but a collusive industrywide ban violated all his free-market beliefs. He pointed out, however, that many writers, using pseudonyms, did find employment during the blacklist period. That escape hatch would not have been available, he argued, if the government owned the movie industry and there was no free market for talent.

Friedman did not inveigh against all government action, pointing out more than once that he was no anarchist; but in his worldview, government was not the savior, not our paternalistic uncle who could solve all social problems, but a necessary element in the good society so long as it was limited—and a potential danger if it was not held in check. "Government is essential," he wrote, "both as a forum for determining 'the rules of the game' and as an umpire to interpret and enforce the rules."

All this was new to me, intellectually stimulating, exciting. I was intrigued as well by the specific application of Friedman's doctrine to the current scene. He was against subsidies for agriculture, a subject that, understandably, had never preoccupied me. He also was opposed to import quotas of all sorts and to other constraints on international trade. But I was both startled and impressed by Friedman's assault on the federal old-age retirement program: "The citizen of the United States who is compelled by law to devote something like 10 percent of his income to the purchase of a particular kind of retirement contract, administered by the government, is being deprived of a corresponding part of his personal freedom." This was a new thought, and I found it persuasive, though there was no immediate threat to an impecunious student. Of more compelling personal interest was Friedman's strong opposition to the military draft in peacetime.

Recently, I've looked again at the book. It's amazing how many of Friedman's specific points have become part of the conventional wisdom. Farm subsidies have no intellectual defenders, though they still get enacted by Congress. The predominant sentiment in the country is for free trade. Deregulation of the transport industries has advanced mightily since Friedman wrote. So has the deregulation of banking. Rent control has been abolished almost everywhere, except in New York City and a few other places. Many proposals have been floated to reform Social Security pensions. And, of course, the peacetime draft has long since been abolished.

My first reading of *Capitalism and Freedom* had left me so enthusiastic that I wrote Friedman a fan letter. He responded with a reading list. And I applied to the Chicago business school and was accepted.

Money was tight and I traveled to Chicago by bus, an experience only for the young and hardy. When I had my interview with George P. Shultz, dean of the business school (and later Secretary of State in the Reagan administration), he persuaded me to cross-register in the economics department, inasmuch as I had gotten through college without even an introductory course in the field. It was good advice, for a strong background in microeconomics is essential if one is to study finance seriously. I also believe that a grounding in microeconomics is desirable for managers in accounting, marketing, and production, and it is especially useful in planning strategy. Among the courses that I took in the economics department were Milton Friedman's on money, Al Rees's on labor, and Harry Johnson's on international trade. In the business school, I was greatly impressed by George Stigler's course on industrial organization. I also took a fine arts course. I was trying to broaden myself.

At the outset, however, I found that I was often at a disadvantage in classes in the business school. My ignorance of economic concepts can be gauged by the fact that I initially thought that the word "marginal" meant "limited" or "minimal." By contrast, my fellow students included some of the best and brightest stars of the next generation of scholars in finance, all of whom had taken many courses in economics. Listening to the lectures, I could usually understand the various details but not how they fitted together. I was lost in the trees and could not see the forest. Then one day, the disassembled pieces would come together, and I understood the whole picture. But it was a slow process.

While I was an MBA candidate at Chicago, I was not initially aware that I was living through a revolution in financial theory. My exposure came through a course on the theory and practice of corporate finance, given by Merton Miller. Miller took off from what became the famous Modigliani-Miller (or M&M) propositions, which first appeared in an article by him and Franco Modigliani in a scholarly journal in 1958. Years later, both were to win Nobel prizes. The M&M propositions asserted that in a perfect world (without taxes but with costless information), the value of a firm did not depend on its capital structure, that is, its ratio of debt to equity. Instead, a firm's value was determined by its likely success in managing its assets, which were measured not by its accounting income but rather by its economic income. Even with the modifications introduced by an imperfect world, the same principle held up quite well. In a later academic paper on dividend policy, published in 1961, just a year before I enrolled in graduate school, Modigliani and Miller demonstrated that whether a company paid dividends was as irrelevant as its capital structure to how it was valued in the stock market. Once again, a firm's value was determined by its prospects and its economic income.

These concepts were revolutionary at the time, though they have since become widely accepted. When Miller and Modigliani first published their articles, the conventional wisdom was just the opposite. With no dissent from the academic community, investment bankers were continually advising firms how they could raise their stock price by rejiggering their capital structure or manipulating their dividend policy. In his classes, Professor Miller clearly saw the situation as an intellectual battleground. I remember he would draw a vertical line on the blackboard and write "M&M" as a heading to the left of the line and "T" to the right of the line. Then he started to list different items under each heading. Never hesitant to ask questions, I raised my hand. "I don't understand what 'T' stands for," I said. "Them," Miller responded. He was always at war with "them."

As I have said, I was often lost in the thicket of new concepts and asked too many questions. One day Miller got fed up with me and urged me to visit the bin outside the dean's office, where there was an accordion file folder for each student. I still remember his exact words: "There will be a derringer in the file for you. Please keep pulling the trigger until something exciting happens." I was properly chastened, but later Miller gave me a lot of time in his office explaining the concepts that I had difficulty comprehending in class. We became friends and saw a fair amount of each other until his death in 2000 at the age of 77.

An amusing incident occurred years before. I was in Chicago chairing a symposium at which several leading financial economists spoke. I tried to get Miller to speak, but he was adamant in his refusal. He finally agreed to attend the luncheon that followed. When the lunch began, I mentioned his presence to the audience and asked the group to stand to do him honor—a courtesy I had learned from my father whenever one of our teachers entered the room. Miller was then moved to come to the podium and say a few words. He began by stating, "Joel Stern was always one of my favorite students." I was floored. My contemporaries at Chicago had somewhat better memories. A few years ago, the business school had a drive to endow a chair in honor of Merton Miller. Stern Stewart & Co. contributed $100,000, and I went to the celebratory dinner in Chicago. Among the speakers was my schoolmate Myron Scholes, who had gone on to make outstanding contributions to finance theory and to become a Nobel laureate. Scholes made some flattering references to the success of Stern Stewart & Co., but felt compelled to point out that I had not been a very good student. I forgave him, and I've never forgotten that the ideas I absorbed at the Chicago Graduate School of Business became the foundation of whatever business success I've enjoyed.

I also learned a good deal from my fellow students, a most talented lot. The dormitory had a study hall, where we often gathered in the afternoon to hash over what we had been exposed to in class. Most of the others were a year or two ahead of me, some of them going for their Ph.D.s; but we were enrolled in many of the same courses. Among my fellow students were Hans Stoll, who in later years became the star of the Vanderbilt University Owen Graduate School of Management; John Gould, who went on to become dean of the Chicago business school; Marshall Blume, who lived across the hall from me and who for some years has been an outstanding professor of finance at the Wharton School. I've already mentioned Myron Scholes, and among the others who later made signal contributions to finance theory were Michael Jensen (University of Rochester and Harvard), Eugene Fama (University of Chicago) and Richard Roll (UCLA).

I knew poverty for the first and only time at Chicago. I can't say it was an ennobling experience, but it was easy to take when young and vigorous and possessed of seemingly realistic dreams. I had resolved to get through graduate school without being a burden on my parents. I had a full-tuition scholarship, and I got some modest help from my father; but I was largely dependent on my savings and summer employment. Throughout my college years, I had spent my summers working "in advertising," as I told people. Actually, I was an itinerant salesman of window decals, trudging around the city with a 70-pound bag of decals—Fresh Produce, Frozen Goods, Dairy Products, that sort of thing. My customers were grocery stores, meat markets, convenience stores, just as long as they carried White Rose tea or other food. When I got an order, I would haul out my roller and pan, fill it with water, and slap on the adhesive paper. It was my first selling experience, and I grew pretty adept at persuading shopkeepers to plaster their windows with abandon. My employer, of course, was the White Rose tea company, whose product was also represented by one or more decals that I managed to include. An inspector from the company later surveyed my handiwork and paid me on a square-footage basis on top of a small minimum guarantee. I was paid double if I managed to affix two rows of decals on a window, thereby positioning the White Rose decals closer to eye level.

On one occasion, an indulgent Spanish-speaking shopkeeper, who said he was delighted to help a student, gave me carte blanche with his windows while he worked in the back room of his shop. I affixed several rows of decals, with generous representation of White Rose Tea and White Rose Foods. I was standing on the sidewalk, admiring my handiwork, when the proprietor came storming out. I had covered so much of his windows that it was completely dark inside the store. But the decals had dried and it would have been a heroic task to scrape them off. So I fled, with him shouting after me.

Of necessity, I was on a tight budget when I got to Chicago. I was able to afford rent in the graduate men's dormitory. Eating, however, was a problem. I adhered to the rules of kashruth, which meant that I could not eat in a student mess. I also could not afford full board at the home of a woman who served kosher meals to observant students, except for the sabbath meal, which cost $2. My solution, during my first year, was to cook my own meals at the graduate men's dormitory.

My provisions cost me $7 a week (remember that this was

1962–1963). This meant many cans of tuna, but it also allowed for milk and eggs. I normally prepared my dinner around 6 P.M. and frequently cooked a Spanish omelet. Everybody in the dorm was aware when Joel was cooking, for the lights would dim when I switched on my 1500-watt hot plate. My major logistical problem was that I lacked a refrigerator, so I kept my milk on the outside window sill. This worked for a time; but the first frost of the season, much to my surprise, left me with a frozen, cracked bottle, with the cream protruding from the top. I had a milk popsicle.

I finally decided to buy a used refrigerator for $38. I got permission to install it in an alcove near the television room on the first floor of the dormitory, thereby providing my schoolmates with a convenient place to keep their beer cold. I quickly turned a profit, for I rented out space to my fellow students for $12 per half shelf per academic quarter. I collected rent on nine and one-half shelves, which gave me a gross of $432 for a full year. That was my first successful enterprise. With that towering return on investment, I was convinced that the free enterprise system worked just fine.

Later on, I had a major windfall. I opened a can of tuna one day and found slivers of glass inside. At the time, I was taking a course in business law with Professor Jacob Weissman. I telephoned him to ask whether the doctrine of manufacturer's liability, which we had been studying in class, applied in this case. Most assuredly, said the professor. I sent my complaint to the company and was ultimately rewarded with a check for $200.

I had something of a social life during the day, by way of bull sessions with my fellow students, but not at night, for I had a huge amount to study and, more to the point, I didn't have the money to date. But for some unaccountable reason, my dormmates elected me social chairman of the men's graduate dormitory. I was willing, but I asked, "What do you want me to do?" The response was clear: "Get women." The idea was to have a discotheque dance in the dorm, for we were in no position to hire a band. The dormitory president advised me to recruit dance partners from a local nursing school. "Nurses know what to do," I was told. The mission was more easily accomplished than I would have thought. We hired a bus, and on the appointed evening, a busload of eager dancers arrived at the dorm. The men and women quickly paired off; and when I checked the bus 15 minutes later, it was empty. And not many people were dancing.

The dance was so successful that a few months later I was asked to arrange another one. This time my recruiting effort might be called serendipitous. To get some exercise, I had acquired a used three-speed bicycle and was in the habit of riding back and forth from the university on the south side of Chicago to the Loop. At one point, I set myself the goal of making a round-trip to Northwestern University in Evanston, Illinois, which I had never visited—a distance of about 20 miles each way. I trained for a couple of weeks, gradually extending my daily stint. On the appointed day, I peddled to Northwestern and wheeled into a quadrangle surrounded by what appeared to be sorority houses, for there were so many girls walking around. I came to a stop, rather breathless, in front of one of the prettiest young women I had ever glimpsed. "Why are you here? Who are you?" she asked, pleasantly enough.

I replied, "I'm the social chairman of the men's graduate dormitory of the University of Chicago Business School, and I'm here under orders to quote get women unquote."

"What do you have in mind?" she asked.

"One busload will be enough." I told her about the dance, and she said she'd try to help. In the end, 53 coeds were bused down to Chicago. We kept the bus all night so that no one could claim that our guests were stranded, but no one required transport until the following morning, when I heard a large commotion in the lobby as our guests bid us goodbye. My fellow students assured me that I could remain social chairman for as long as I cared to.

With the approach of summer vacation at the end of my first

year, I once again confronted a desperate need for money. I went to the placement office and asked if there were any summer jobs available. Not in Chicago, I was told, but there were some in New York. "That'd be okay," I said, "I have a place to stay." A short while later, Barry Sullivan came to Chicago to recruit for the Chase Manhattan Bank. Sullivan, a former star basketball player at Georgetown University and an impressive physical presence as well as a man of great charm, had gotten a Chicago MBA a few years before and was now a vice president at Chase Manhattan. Years later he was to become chairman and CEO of the First National Bank of Chicago. Not the least of his attractiveness was his penchant for blunt language and quick decisions.

"Why do you want to come to work for the Chase Manhattan Bank?" Sullivan asked.

"I haven't a clue," I said, guessing that he would appreciate candor. "Can I tell you the truth? I need the money."

"You're hired," said Sullivan.

It was not too much of a risk, for the job was only for the summer. I worked directly for Sullivan, on the seventh floor of the bank's headquarters at 1 Chase Manhattan Plaza. I handled several small projects for him, and at the end of the summer he offered me a full-time job when I got my MBA in 1964. That launched me on my career line.

3

Rebel Banker

When Barry Sullivan made his job offer, I naturally inquired about salary. "$7,200 a year," said Sullivan, whereupon I asked for $8,500. He seemed a bit startled and asked why. Said I, "If you pay me $8,500, all of the senior management of the bank will know who I am because I'll be the overpaid one. I'll have visibility." And he agreed.

My reasoning was not as presumptuous as it sounds. I was hired for the Special Development Program—Chase's name for its executive training program, from which the bank's future leaders were expected to emerge. (Tom Labrecque, for example, was enrolled in the program when I was and ultimately became the chief executive of the bank.) The trainees were routinely exposed to every activity of the bank as well as to the top brass, many of whom addressed our group and responded to questions. They saw enough of us to make individual assessments. Little wonder that I was determined to make an impression.

At the outset, however, Barry Sullivan was concerned that I might be making the wrong impression. The problem was the unofficial dress code. When I was hired, I had but two outfits that I thought appropriate for business. One was a brown sharkskin suit that was almost in shreds, the other was a blue blazer and gray slacks that I always wore with a bright yellow vest, to which I was passionately devoted. Barry vetoed both outfits.

"What should I wear?" I asked. "Look around you," he said. So I went to Brooks Brothers and told a salesman that I worked for the Chase bank (he looked skeptical when I said that) and needed the proper attire. I bought six dark suits—three for winter wear, three for summer. Now when I dressed for work, I had that reassuring sense of belonging that wearing a uniform brings.

Life at Chase was very structured. After the Special Development Program came the credit training program, designed to turn out commercial lending officers, the largest executive strata of the bank. It was an intensive program that largely involved on-the-job training. We also took exams in accounting, corporate finance, and credit analysis, among other subjects; anyone who failed an exam had to endure a makeup course in the subject and undergo another exam. At Chicago, I had taken two courses in accounting—one in managerial accounting and the other in cost accounting—and had done well. But I was something of a smart aleck when I took the Chase accounting test and I flunked. Instead of giving the answers that I knew were expected, I quarreled with the premises of the questions and couldn't repress my disdain for using accounting concepts to determine the value of an asset or a company.

But I had learned my lesson. I went through the tedium of another accounting course and passed the second time, giving the required conventional answers. I did the same thing in the finance and economics exams, each of which was a trial for me. The macroeconomics exam, for example, was based on Keynesian premises; and by this time, I had become a budding monetarist, due to the Chicago influence.

The on-the-job credit training was interesting, though. Each trainee worked under the supervision of a senior credit analyst, studying loan requests from a variety of companies and assessing credit risks. These were real companies, not hypothetical ones; and when the analysis was finished, the supervisor presented it to the bank lending officer responsible for that credit, with the trainee tagging along to hear the appraisal. Our assignments involved three types of companies: a financial service firm, a manufacturing company, and a diverse category that might include a high-tech firm or a retail operation. From time to time, each of us would have to stand in front of a classroom and present an analysis. Presiding over the session was the bank official who was the second in command of the credit department. These sessions were popularly known as "pit referrals"—a metaphor for being thrown into a lion's pit, to be torn limb from limb.

Most of my colleagues survived the hazards and were appointed lending officers. Some of my friends were hired by other banks, for the Chase program was widely admired. But when I graduated from the program in 1966, I ran as fast as I could from commercial lending. That was not at all what I wanted to do. I was eager for a job where I could think about the big issues; and I had the good fortune to be assigned to Chase's corporate finance advisory group, a small operation called Corporate Financial Research. All told, there were only about five people there, headed by Harry Abplanalp, serving a small group of companies, doing very complicated analysis, much too complicated and time-consuming for the commercial lending officers to undertake. Our group dealt with all kinds of strategic financial questions, anything from a company's capital structure and debt capacity to the valuation of a potential merger. All this was provided as a free service. For once, my education in Chicago was relevant.

But I am getting ahead of myself. In 1966, when I was still in the credit training program, I married Karen Darwick. The marriage lasted 14 years, ending in divorce; so it can hardly be regarded as one of my (or our) successes. But it produced one child, Erik Daniel, who was born on my thirtieth birthday. (The "k" in our son's name, incidentally, reflects his mother's admiration for the celebrated psychologist, the late Erik Eriksen.) Erik is a remarkably gifted and energetic young man who, since he was 29, has been a senior vice president of Stern Stewart. When he joined our firm after earning his MBA, I told my partners that when we climbed a mountain, Erik would climb Mount Everest; when we climbed Mount Everest, Erik would climb its steepest slope.

Karen and I had met on October 2, 1965, and were engaged to be married six weeks later. A good deal of chance was involved in our coming together, as I guess is often the case in these matters. I had a friend named Stanley Richelson, who was dating a girl named Joan. Joan's best friend was Karen, whom Stanley described as gorgeous and brilliant. She was a college student who had recently transferred from the University of Wisconsin to New York and who was living with her parents in Riverdale, the upscale section of the Bronx. Due to the geographic switch, Karen was, as they say, "available." So, as it happened, was I. Stanley urged a double date. I tended to shy away from blind dates, but I finally agreed.

At the appointed time, I showed up at Karen's home. When her mother opened the door, I unwittingly ingratiated myself by exclaiming, "I'm afraid you're not properly dressed for the evening." To which her mother replied, "You must be kidding. I really like you!"

We had a pleasant evening, in the course of which I (ever the proselytizer) suggested that if we were to continue to see each other, she should read Milton Friedman's *Capitalism and Freedom*. After all, we could not spend all our time just talking about pop culture and trivia. She agreed to read the book.

When I took Karen home that night, she started to open the door, only to find her father behind it. "What do you think of my daughter?" he barked. "Do you want to see her again?"

"Yes, I do," I said, startled by the frontal assault.

"If you do, then tomorrow morning we'll play tennis at nine o'clock. You be right here."

I looked at Karen, who smiled. "Are you going to be there?" I asked.

She said she would, and I agreed, but pointed out that I played a poor game. That was my introduction to my future father-in-law and his passion for tennis, a game he played two or three times a week, beating the pants off men half his age.

The following morning, I appeared on time and the three of us repaired to the courts in a public park. Once again, I mentioned that I didn't play tennis very well. Darwick served first. I swung wildly at the first ball and missed. The second one I didn't even see. He waved me to the net. "Don't tell me you tell the truth too!" he exclaimed. He then announced that he would give me tennis lessons.

Under his tutelage, you had to do everything in sequence and then remember the sequence—stand sideways, racket back, knees bent, swing up to hit the ball and follow through. At one point, I said to him, "You know, I was watching Stan Smith play. He didn't stand sideways, he didn't bring the racket back." And Darwick said to me, "When you get as good as Stan Smith, you can play tennis any way you like. While you are playing with me, you might as well learn how to play the game properly. And don't talk so much."

Karen and I got on well. She even read *Capitalism and Freedom* and made some polite noises about it, surely a token of affection. I fell in love with her not instantly but rapidly. I've always liked bright, intelligent women who were interested in serious subjects and whose conversation deserved close attention. I do like to listen, almost as much as I like to talk. And Karen was beautiful, never discount that, there was a strong mutual attraction. I was just utterly captivated. I felt I had found my mate for life.

When we decided to get married, I called her father on Thanksgiving eve. I told him that I was an old-fashioned guy and was asking his permission for his daughter's hand in marriage. "How does she feel about it?" he wanted to know.

"I think she's in favor of the idea," I assured him.

"How did it happen?" Darwick inquired.

I explained, "We went to see *Doctor Zhivago* last Saturday night. It was three and a half hours long. In fact, we want the musical theme from *Doctor Zhivago* to be the musical theme of our wedding."

Darwick's response was, "Do you intend to improve your tennis?" I assured him that I did, and he gave us his blessing. Later, I was surprised that he did not ask me to sign a contract.

Unhappily, as I said, the marriage did not turn out well. We never really spoke to each other; we did not communicate on the deepest level. By that I mean that we were never able to identify with the emotional condition of the other person. I was less than enthusiastic about Karen's academic aspirations, as she accumulated advanced degrees in history, Russian literature, and, finally, psychology. I did not understand what drove her. And she was not particularly empathetic with my frustrations and later triumphs as an iconoclastic young banker at Chase.

Breaking up was painful for both of us. We were both concerned with avoiding any harmful impact on Erik, who was then nine. We were determined not to use him as a listening post for any resentments each of us may have felt. Karen had custody, but I saw Erik frequently, on weekends and holidays. I probably saw more of him than if we had remained married, given the extent of my travels. The point is that I now exerted myself to see my son. After I built my house in East Hampton, Erik visited frequently, whether I had guests or not.

And Erik flourished. He had an adventuresome adolescence. While attending Horace Mann, a prep school in New York, he spent a summer on his own initiative at the St. Barnabas School in a suburb of Johannesburg, on the border of Soweto, where most of the students were black. He made a movie about the school and later submitted it as part of his application to Brown University. After he received his bachelor's degree, he enrolled in the business school at the University of Chicago, spent a year, and then decided it was wise to have some business experience before getting his MBA. He went to Paris and took a short course in political science and contemporary history at a French university, which led to a research job at the French national railways, the SNCF, and then employment with the bank, Credit Lyonnais. His MBA came in 1997, after he spent a summer at the Rotterdam School of Management, an exchange school with Chicago. Then he joined Stern Stewart in our London office. Three years later, he was running it.

As for Karen, before long she found her metier as a psychologist. She specializes in the problems of adolescents with learning disabilities and enjoys a thriving practice. And I finally learned to play a decent game of tennis. We both take pleasure in the success of our son.

Despite the marital tension, I had been forging ahead in those early years at Chase, though raises were modest—$1,000 or $2,000 a year, as was typical of a commercial bank. Abplanalp's advisory group held to conventional views as to how the stock market values companies, but I was given a hearing and eventually allowed to try out my heresy on clients. The conventional view, for example, was that earnings per share (EPS) was the ultimate determinant of a company's share price, the engine that drove value. If EPS increased, the share price would rise in tandem, like an automaton (the price/earnings ratio being assumed to be constant), unless, of course, the whole market was in a downdraft. My view, derived from Modigliani and Miller, was that the focus on EPS was misguided, for there were so many ways that a company could manipulate its EPS. It was far better to concentrate on a company's economic performance, beginning with its cash flow. (I later developed the concept of free cash flow, to which I alluded in the first chapter.)

My colleagues at the bank believed, as did most of Wall Street at the time, that the markets could be fooled by accounting manipulations. Playing tricks with the numbers—legal tricks—was thus a legitimate pursuit for consultants. There were many ways to do this. One popular technique was "trade loading," in which a company persuaded its customers to accept more goods than they wanted in a specific quarter (the seller financing the inventory) in order to boost the seller's quarterly earnings. Another gimmick, for the purpose of "smoothing out" earnings, involved a company putting excessive reserves on its balance sheet (for, say, bad debts or defective merchandise) in one quarter, thereby lowering earnings below what they otherwise would have been, and then reversing the process in another quarter, which had the effect of converting some of the excess reserves into profit at a time when the company wanted to show a healthy increase in earnings.

By contrast, I did not believe that the market could easily be fooled. I advanced the view that market prices were set at the margin by the most sophisticated and knowledgeable investors—I later called them the "lead steers"—who spotted the gimmickry and focused on the underlying economic reality of the firm. My colleagues scoffed at the notion. They believed that market prices were set by the weighted average action of all investors. This was like asking a herd of cattle where they were heading and listening to all to gauge their future direction. My view was that prices responded to marginal behavior, the voice of the lead steer. In later years, this might be Warren Buffett unexpectedly buying Coca-Cola, Peter Lynch acquiring Hanes, George Long of Oppenheimer Capital selling Kodak, or South Africa's Allan Gray doing anything at all.

My colleagues and I also had our differences on questions of capital structure. Our group frequently advised clients on appropriate debt/equity ratios. The bank, of course, had a vested interest in encouraging customers to assume more debt—lending money, after all, was its principal business. But there was a genuine intellectual difference between my colleagues and myself on the debt issue. They held to the simplistic view that the overall cost of capital declined to the extent that lower-cost debt replaced higher-cost equity. (The cheaper cost of debt, of course, derived from the tax deductibility of interest.) For example, let's say a slice of a firm's equity capital (bearing a cost of 12 percent) was replaced by debt costing 8 percent. The firm certainly saved money, but it didn't save 4 percent, for the greater debt burden increased the risk borne by shareholders—and increased risk, axiomatically, raises the cost of equity capital. Okay, said my detractors, but raised by how much? You can't quantify the increased risk. Not so, said I, referring them to the Miller-Modigliani proposition number two: determinants of the cost of equity capital.

We had other differences involving balance sheet items. They favored the standard practice of keeping operating leases off the balance sheet, another popular manipulation. I favored capitalizing the leases and putting them on the balance sheet, writing off their value year by year until the leases expired. Their preferred practice understated the firm's assets and thereby showed a higher return on net assets (RONA) than my method did. But which gave a truer picture?

It was an uphill struggle to persuade my colleagues of my heretical views, and I never succeeded with most of them. I gradually began to understand the threat that new ideas presented in a placid, self-satisfied culture. The commercial banking industry was one in which the risk/reward ratio for employees was heavily weighted against the assumption of risk. It was a highly regulated industry at the time, with banks limited, for example, in the range of their activities and in the interest they could pay on their deposits. Moreover, there was no danger in that industry of poor performance carrying the threat of a hostile takeover, an unheard-of phenomenon at the time. Boards of directors were also tolerant of poor performance, so long as other banks performed poorly, too.

Individuals were certainly not motivated to be innovative, because of both the atmosphere in which they worked and the way they were paid. Compensation was heavily weighted toward fixed pay—usually 85 percent, with a mere 15 percent in variable pay supposedly based on performance (but an employee had to goof badly to be denied the annual bonus). A successful new idea received a modest reward, whereas failure could threaten one's job. With variable pay so modest, the only way to get a substantial raise was to enlarge one's domain. In the case of lending officers, that meant increasing one's "total footings"—the odd phrase for loan volume. (A footing, I discovered, was the sum at the bottom of a column of figures.) But here again, caution was the watchword, for if a loan went sour, it was a black mark against the lending officer.

Despite the inhospitable setting at Chase, I restlessly pressed ahead, possessed of that missionary zeal that has never left me, as well as more than a touch of youthful arrogance. By 1969, I was allowed to call on some of the bank's clients, accompanied by a senior lending officer. I was also allowed to charge a fee, having persuaded Abplanalp that we devalued our product by giving it away free. The first fee involved a significant consulting contract with Bethlehem Steel. I was shepherded to the company's headquarters in Pennsylvania by Bob Blomquist, a Chase vice president who was in charge of commercial lending in the Pennsylvania and Ohio territory. At the time, the bank divided up the country geographically rather than by industry group, which came later.

I had an interesting relationship with Blomquist, a man whose physical bulk lent weight to his authoritative, deliberate tone but who was amiable enough to sustain dissent. He had taught the makeup course in accounting that I had been compelled to take. After I passed the exam, Blomquist and I had continued to meet and to argue about my newfangled notions.

On this occasion, Blomquist had arranged for us to call on Bethlehem Steel's treasurer, who graciously consented to give me a hearing. My goal was to sell our services, which did not sit well with Blomquist. Bethlehem was a client with a large depository relationship with Chase. It had also taken out large loans, a portion of which—perhaps as much as 20 percent—was left in the bank as "compensating balances." Blomquist was concerned that I do nothing to jeopardize the relationship. "You're not going to ask them for a fee, are you?" he demanded. I replied, "If we give it away for nothing, as part of the depository relationship, he won't put any value on it. We have to charge them a fee." Blomquist then adopted a stern tone:

"What you'll do is this: You'll make your presentation. And then he'll probably say, 'What is this going to cost me?' After hearing from you, if he then says, 'Oh, you've got to be kidding. After all, we have this depository relationship,' you'll keep your mouth shut. Or you'll say, 'You're right, it's free.' Is that clear?" I uttered a weak assent.

The scenario went as Blomquist had anticipated. I made my presentation and almost immediately the treasurer asked, "What will this cost me?" I said either $5,000 or $10,000, I forget which. The treasurer looked startled. But I did not keep my mouth shut. Instead, I blurted out, "Sir, the reason we're visiting you first is because you have this extraordinary depository relationship with our bank. We would not even be here if we did not have this relationship, and that's why we're offering this outstanding service to you."

In my imagination, I thought I heard the thud of Blomquist's body hitting the floor. But what I actually heard was the treasurer saying, "Good response. Good idea. We'll do it."

When we got outside, I looked at Blomquist. He looked like a man who had died and come alive. "Are you okay?" I asked.

"I thought you had lost the Bethlehem relationship," he said.

And I had learned something else about the risk/reward ratio: I had been emboldened because I never thought there was much danger of losing Bethlehem, and the potential reward of landing the contract was worth whatever risk existed—to Chase as well as to me.

In 1969 I got another break. Without conceding that he agreed with me (I doubt that he ever did while we were both at Chase), Harry Abplanalp saw the virtue of getting a wider forum for my views. Thus was born the series of two-day Financial Policy Management Forums that continue to this day at Stern Stewart, though they now occupy but a single day and I am not the only speaker.

The idea behind the forums was to offer an extended airing of my views in order to persuade senior executives to experiment with a novel approach. There was no way of convincing top managers to abandon long-held views by exposing them to a single lecture. It was a radically new and complex world that they were being asked to enter, and it was necessary to immerse them in the new material for an extended period to make an impact—much like the "total immersion" courses to teach a foreign language when quick results are needed. The audience that we reached consisted of the top financial managers of companies—chief financial officers, controllers, treasurers, senior planning officers, and even CEOs on many occasions. No other bank was offering anything like this intellectual immersion and it was viewed as a good way to distinguish ourselves from our rivals, a standard marketing strategy.

We held the seminars in conference centers in Westchester and on Long Island, New York. Generally, about 30 people attended, 2 or 3 per company. Sessions ran seven hours a day, with a lunch break and morning and afternoon coffee breaks. I did all the lecturing, a marathon effort that still surprises me, less because of the stamina involved than for the fact that the audience did not decamp.

By 1969, I was well prepared for these exertions, for I already had considerable experience talking on my feet. In 1965, after my first year at Chase, I had begun teaching night classes at the City College of New York, an assignment that came about unexpectedly. One day I had received a telephone call from Henry Villard, head of the economics department of CCNY. Villard said they needed someone to teach the entire sequence of courses in economics to students attending night classes. I had been recommended by one of my teachers at Chicago. I asked why the regular faculty could not handle the chore, and his reply was a classic: "It's not safe here at night" (CCNY is in Harlem, at 138th Street and Convent Avenue). The presumed hazards did not faze me and I was attracted by an academic connection—an attraction that has never left me. I also very much wanted to hone my communications skills.

Before accepting, however, I felt compelled to tell Villard about my draft status. Previously, I had had student deferments, but I was now 1A and thought I might be called up the following September.

"No, you won't be," said Professor Villard. He would write my draft board, stating that I was essential to his operation, for he had no one else to teach night classes. The draft board was indulgent and I received two deferments, by which time I was no longer eligible for the draft. I taught at CCNY from 1965 to 1970. Meantime, other youngsters were dispatched to the jungles of Vietnam. I don't claim the system was fair.

Night class at CCNY was a good place to practice those communications skills. Students worked during the day and were not in the most receptive state to study the dismal science when they got to class. Most of them had no interest in the subject but were in attendance to fulfill requirements. Those in the back row tended to fall asleep. I met the challenge through a variety of techniques. One was a sudden rise in decibel count. I would be going along in a moderate tone and then would suddenly emphasize a point by shouting. That would wake them up. At times, I hammed it up with extravagant gestures. I learned to watch my audience carefully, alert to signs of flagging attention. Then I would toss in a joke or suddenly point a finger at a student and ask a question.

I learned that the art of holding an audience's attention was similar to retaining the attention of a single individual—you watched facial expression and body language for any sign of incipient boredom, then swiftly changed pace. Indeed, it is often easier to hold an audience than a single listener, for the audience is usually rooting for the speaker to carry it off and squirms at any hesitancy or gaffe. For the same reason, the mild joke that only gets a faint smile from a single listener will elicit a loud guffaw from a crowd.

So I was quite prepared for the first management forum—the announced subject was "Analytical Methods in Financial Planning"—which was held in November 1969. Over the course of the two days, five main subjects were covered: (1) the determinants of value, (2) capital structure planning, (3) acquisition pricing and financing, (4) financial communication, and (5) setting corporate goals.

The first day's session covered the deficiencies of the accounting model of the firm as compared with the economic model. I highlighted the drawbacks of earnings per share and growth by accounting profit as predictors of future share value, and I devoted a lot of attention to the question of what fundamentally creates value. I stressed that the value of a corporation is determined by two factors. The first involved expected future corporate returns (the quality of management), as compared with the second factor, the required rate of return, also known as the cost of capital. Value is enhanced, of course, to the extent that the former outweighs the latter. This second factor is also directly related to the risk involved in the enterprise. If managers assumed more risk in order to increase returns, the required rate of return would also rise, for it is axiomatic that greater risk requires higher rewards. Both are keenly watched by the "lead steers" patrolling the market place.

The question of capital structure—what is the optimum mix of debt and equity and the advantages and disadvantages of different kinds of debt—absorbed a good deal of time. We covered the tax break that makes debt capital cheaper than equity, an advantage that is reduced somewhat, as mentioned before, by the enhanced risk that debt brings. There was also extended treatment of the distinction between a company's growth and its expansion. Simply put, growth occurs when the increase in corporate returns is greater than the cost of capital, whereas expansion is defined as an increase in returns at the cost-of-capital level or below it. The cost of capital—the rate of return that the market demands—is thus the benchmark, with growth companies invariably enjoying higher price/earnings ratios (P/Es) than do companies that merely expand. Expanding firms can only command a P/E equal to the reciprocal of the cost of capital. Thus, a 10 percent cost of capital yields a P/E of 10. If less than the cost of capital is earned, the P/E is correspondingly reduced.

The sessions also dealt with the technical question of how to measure risk, the need for a "target capital structure" as a corporate goal, ways to improve financial communication so that the market knows what the company is doing, and the question of the extent to which markets are "efficient," among other topics. Starting in 1972, a good deal of time was devoted to the subject of free cash flow, the calculation of which I will explain in due course.

In addition to these management forums at which several companies were represented, we also held two-day forums for a single company, usually attended by the CEO and members of the executive committee, in which I zeroed in on the particular concerns of the host company. We called these our "in-house" forums, which inevitably meant that the multicompany sessions became known around our shop as "out-house" forums.

Before long, I was presenting my views in print as well as on the podium. In 1972, I met Jude Wanniski, best known as one of the journalistic celebrants of "supply side" economics. At that time, Jude was an editorial writer on the *Wall Street Journal*. He was interested in my views on financial strategy, and he introduced me to Robert L. Bartley, the editor of the *Journal*'s editorial page. Bartley suggested that I write an article for his page, which duly appeared on December 18, 1972, with the title "Let's Abandon Earnings Per Share." I made my standard arguments about the inadequacy of EPS as a measure of corporate performance. "Determining the merit of corporate policies by their impact on per-share earnings is fraught with danger," I wrote. "EPS is too often a misleading indicator that can result in costly decisions that frequently shortchange the common shareholder." Heretical language at the time—hence, the prominence given the article at the top of the editorial page.

The lead editorial that day dealt with my piece. It did not dispute the logic of my analysis but rather its relevance, questioning whether markets were truly efficient. "Do today's 'sophisticated' investors," it asked, "really depend on a keen appreciation of the underlying value that results from economic efficiency, or instead does their 'sophistication' take the form of 'recognizing' that it is all a psychological game, and that the trick is to spot the next fad a week earlier than the rest?" I hardly minded the disagreement, for I was eager for any available platform—and the *Wall Street Journal* was certainly among the best. (Both the article and the editorial are reprinted in the appendix to this volume.)

There was also an unexpected and welcome consequence of my article: a call from Freddy Fisher, the editor of the *Financial Times* of London, asking me to contribute an article to his paper. Instead, I proposed five articles, to appear every other Friday for ten weeks. He agreed. Out of this arrangement, which started in February 1973, came a total of 96 articles. I also began publishing pieces in the *Commercial and Financial Chronicle* of New York and the *Straits Times* of Singapore and, in the late 1970s, on the op-ed page of the *Wall Street Journal*. Exposure of this sort was worth infinitely more than even a multi-million-dollar advertising campaign.

These short articles were an effort to popularize the themes I covered in the seminars. Several of them were excerpted, somewhat modified, in a paperback book—the "blue book," from its cover—published by the Chase Manhattan Bank under the title *Analytical Methods in Financial Planning* by Joel M. Stern, with the copyright retained by me. I covered such subjects as "The Real Benefits of Debt Financing," "How to Calculate the True Cost of Capital," and "Rapid Earnings Growth Is No Guarantee of a High P/E." After Stern Stewart was founded, we republished the book.

I trust the reader will indulge me if I give a bit of the flavor of these outpourings, which were not meant to be light reading. In the last named article, I dealt with the paradoxical fact that many companies that report rapid increases in earnings do not enjoy a high P/E. I wrote that "analysts and management are often baffled by the 'irrationality' of the market when such companies sell at low price/earnings ratios. They fail to realize that the market cannot detect any growth and finds no justification for a high P/E. This apparent paradox may cause management to delay a needed equity issue, hoping that the P/E will rise to a more 'realistic' level. It may also deter analysts from recommending a company's shares because they think a company is 'out of favor' with investors."

All this, of course, was a grievous misreading of the underlying dynamics involved. I wrote, "There is no cause-and-effect relationship between rapid earnings growth and a high P/E. Only 'growth' companies, strictly defined, may sell at high P/Es." As I continually told my seminar audiences, the pivotal point was the relationship between the rate of return on net assets and the cost of capital. True growth companies earn rates of return higher than the cost of capital. More precisely, I argued that "the market expects a growth company to earn rates of return on incremental fixed capital that exceed the weighted average cost of debt and equity capital. And the wider the spread between the rate of return and the cost of capital, the greater will be the P/E because investors will be willing to pay a premium for the management's ability."

In an article entitled "How to Calculate the True Cost of Capital," I criticized the prevalent notion on Wall Street that while the cost of debt capital was obviously the interest paid, the cost of equity simply equaled the dividends disbursed. I argued that this was erroneous, for it overlooked the true cost borne by shareholders, which was the opportunity cost of capital—what they could earn by other available investments at the same level of risk. I suggested that the reason security analysts got it wrong was that they preferred working with the available figures put out by public companies. I might have added that most analysts knew little and cared less about financial theory. The true cost of equity, I argued, had to take into account both business risk and the financial risk inherent in leverage, and I provided a formula that would calculate the cost of equity of any company. The next step was to calculate the weighted average cost of total capital, based on the proportion of debt and equity in the mix.

I went on to say, "Because debt is cheaper than equity [largely because of the tax saving], the weighted average cost of capital is invariably less than the cost of common share capital. . . .Which cost of capital is relevant to management in selecting the best investment opportunities for the common shareholder?" The answer: "For companies which employ debt, the weighted average cost of debt and equity is the relevant one because specific funds cannot be identified with specific uses." The reason is simple. If a company used a new infusion of equity to finance a new investment and if equity cost, say, 12 percent, the investment would have to earn at least 12 percent to be justifiable; and many worthwhile projects would be rejected that would be viable if the company used a blended cost-of-capital figure. Similarly, if the debt cost of, say, 4 percent was used in the calculation of what was affordable, uneconomic projects might be undertaken that could not meet the company's true hurdle rate—its blended cost of capital.

Running through these articles, as well as through all my output in this period, was the key concept of free cash flow as the determinant of value. It was particularly useful in measuring the utility of new investment projects, acquisitions, and divestitures. How I lighted on the concept is an interesting story. I might say, incidentally, that this idea, like most of the ideas that I developed in this period, came about as the result of conversations that I had either at Chase Manhattan or with the bank's clients. These people made statements that seemed at such variance with common sense that they could only be true if the markets were systematically irrational or financially unsophisticated or if they were "incomplete markets," that is, not functioning in a way that reflected all the information that was available. But these assumptions about market deficiencies seemed to me to be totally unreasonable when we dealt with the major stock exchanges of the world. More compelling was the assumption that the oft-expressed "truisms" about how the market worked were simply untrue.

How was the concept of free cash flow conceived? I remember

that in one of my early meetings with the treasurer of Bethlehem Steel, the question came up as to how the company's shares were valued by the market. The treasurer suggested that the share price was determined by its dividend yield. At that point, an associate of the treasurer argued that the share price actually reflected the company's earnings, that the market calculated the present value of future earnings, not an uncommon view. Both explanations struck me as wrong. I pointed out that if you took the current dividend plus all the dividends expected in the next 10 years, the sum did not come close to the share price. As for the explanation that earnings were the determining factor, I demurred again, arguing that part of today's earnings had to be reinvested in the business in order to generate future earnings, and thus earnings in themselves could not be the basis of value because the part of today's earnings reinvested would be double counted.

Then I had a flash of memory, suddenly recalling a passage in Miller and Modigliani's famous article on dividends. To determine a company's value, they used the formula "X − I," with "X" standing for earnings and "I" for new investment. So they had the concept long before I did, but they never used the term "free cash flow." I claim authorship of the term, whose value, I think, is both familiarity and clarity.

As a concept, cash flow has been around a very long time. It is derived by taking operating earnings and adding back noncash items like depreciation and amortization and accrued (not cash) taxes. That gives you the actual cash that a company generates. Then comes a significant deduction from that number—the new investment that is necessary to keep the company operating plus any new working capital (the excess of current assets over current liabilities) and any incremental investment to grow the business. What remains after the deductions is "free" cash flow: the amount of cash available for distribution to lenders and shareholders. That is how I define the term; my definition has won wide, though not universal, acceptance.

It follows that if investment equals earnings, there is no free cash flow; but markets assume that in future years the firm will earn a profit on the new investment.

To place a value on the company, you calculate the present value (PV) of the future stream of free cash flows, using the company's cost of capital as the discount rate—the reverse of what is done if you want to know the value 10 or 20 years hence of annual deposits in a savings account at a stipulated rate of interest. Once the PV of a company's free cash flow is calculated, a little arithmetic will express it on a per-share basis. Scrutiny of the stock tables will demonstrate that per-share free cash flow is a much better explanation of share prices than EPS is.

(Years later, at Stern Stewart & Co., we added a further refinement by developing the concept of Economic Value Added [EVA], which is an even more useful measure of value. Although the PV of free cash flow provides a figure for a company's value at a particular time, EVA is a more flexible tool, providing a period-to-period measure of how a company's worth has risen or declined. We will discuss the development of EVA, announced to the world in 1989, in more detail later in this chronicle.)

The purpose of all this scholarly apparatus, of course, was to attract clients. Above all else, mine was a selling job; I was not being paid just to spin theories. Getting my name around, through articles in the financial press and through appearances on Louis Rukeyser's television program "Wall Street Week"—I was a regular panelist for 17 years—was all in furtherance of the cause, though I was no shrinking violet. Meantime, I was progressing at Chase. Two years after I was named a vice president in 1970, I was appointed head of our group, whose name in 1976 was changed to Chase Financial Policy. What had once been a free service to clients was now a significant profit center for the bank.

My relative youth was both an advantage and a handicap. A bright young man forging ahead gets attention, plaudits as well as envy. The disadvantage is that at times one is not taken seriously. I had the special disadvantage of looking younger than my years, a problem that was only overcome with the onset of middle age and an expanding waistline, as well as a greying scenic view from the top. I remember one occasion when I was invited by my superiors to attend a meeting that David Rockefeller had arranged with a group from Firestone Tire & Rubber. I don't remember whether this was before 1969, when Mr. Rockfeller was president and chief operating officer of Chase, or afterward, when he became CEO. In an effort to be punctual, I arrived early and was the first in the conference room. Then the Firestone group walked in, headed by the CEO, whose name I've (understandably) forgotten. When he spotted me, he asked me to fetch some coffee, with milk and sugar. I did so. Then the Chase contingent arrived, headed by Mr. Rockefeller. He made introductions all around, and the Firestone chieftain looked abashed. "Sorry, young man," he said as we shook hands.

I recall two other memorable meetings involving David Rockefeller. The first occurred in 1965 or 1966 when I was still in the credit training program. The bank had a sensible policy of occasionally inviting a trainee to attend a luncheon meeting of the bank's top brass with visiting clients. One day I got the call to attend such a lunch that Mr. Rockefeller was giving in his private dining room for the top executives of the Weyerhaeuser Company. I received the invitation at the last minute, apparently because the intended junior invitee had come down with the flu, but I used what little time I had to scan Weyerhaeuser's annual report and check on its current stock price.

Mr. Rockefeller began lunch by asking George Weyerhaeuser, the company's president, "How's business?" Weyerhaeuser replied, "We're doing real well. We expect to earn profits of such and such, and we expect to earn a return on shareholders' funds in excess of 20 percent after taxes." There were the usual admiring comments from the Chase people, and then there was a bit of a pause. I knew that my role at the meeting was to listen and learn and to keep my mouth shut, but I couldn't restrain myself. So I said, "Do you mind if I ask you a question?" Mild shock appeared on the faces of the Chase people, but Weyerhaeuser was indulgent. "Not at all," he said, whereupon I politely challenged the relevance of the figure for return on shareholder equity.

The colloquy was too long to repeat here—I couched everything in terms of questions—but my point was that the company's assets (mostly timberland) were understated on the balance sheet because they represented low historical numbers (most of the land having been acquired decades earlier) rather than present market value, which was much higher. The result was that shareholder equity was also understated, which produced a higher return on equity than would have been the case if the asset figures were realistic. I pointed out, with a little arithmetic, that the company's share price reflected not the inflated return on equity but rather the market value of the company's acreage. I saw a look of puzzlement on Mr. Rockefeller's face; but Weyerhaeuser said very affably, "That's the way I look at the business, too." So I asked why he had raised the issue of return on equity. He replied, "Well, when you come south of Fourteenth Street in New York, you assume that financial types like you people care about balance sheets and income statements." I replied, "No, we think about market value." Despite my apprehensions, I was not fired.

Some years later, after I was well launched on my consulting career, I was asked to give a talk to the executive committee of the bank. I knew that Mr. Rockefeller, then the CEO, would be present, and I was afraid that once I got into the technical details, he might find the subject too arcane and make an excuse to leave. I was not above flattering the boss, and I did an enterprising but rather curious thing. On a trip to Chicago, I went to the library of the economics department at the University of Chicago and looked up his doctoral dissertation. I took detailed notes and copied word for word the opening paragraph of his conclusion. I knew that Ph.D. candidates labored mightily over the conclusion, for that was the first thing that examiners supposedly read while preparing their barrage of questions. Thus I knew that the boss would recognize the words. So I got up and started to read his opening paragraph. "What has this to do with the subject at hand?" someone said. "Let him finish," Mr. Rockefeller interjected, "he's reading from my doctoral dissertation." And he smiled broadly—he almost laughed, but that would have been too much to expect from this reserved personality. I went away from that meeting knowing that he was unlikely to forget me.

I spent a good deal of time traveling around the country, accompanying loan officers responsible for different geographic areas and trying to sell Chase clients on our advisory services. The introduction by loan officers was invaluable, but there was no grand design to the sales effort. What happened was that Bob Blomquist, after initial resistance, became persuaded by my arguments, and he was also impressed by the success of my sales pitch at Bethlehem Steel. So he recommended me to colleagues responsible for different parts of the country, and we set off.

The first company to sign up for an "in-house" seminar was Pepsi-Cola. That set the pattern. Pepsi had a representative at one of the "out-house" two-day forums who stirred up considerable interest among his colleagues, with the result that I was invited to make a similar presentation to Pepsi's top management. In preparation, one of my associates made a couple of visits to the company to collect the necessary data so that I could tailor my prescriptions to the goals and the financial policy alternatives facing Pepsi. Among the other companies that signed up for the in-house forums were Hewlett-Packard, R. J. Reynolds, Kimberly Clark, Walter E. Heller, American Sugar, and Union Carbide. We charged fees—$5,000 to $15,000— that were modest by present-day standards even after you made the inflation adjustment. But the assignments were short, basically involving our advice as to how the client should shape its financial strategy. We were not retained to help implement our proposals. That only occurred years later after Stern Stewart began marketing EVA. Assignments thereafter ran from three or four months to more than a year.

Some of my Chase clients in the early years became enthusiastic converts to the new doctrines and showed their appreciation by sending me novelty items. From the American Sugar Company I received several boxes of paper-wrapped loose sugar, with my picture on one side and the words "EPS Don't Count" on the other. The CEO of Union Carbide put the same slogan on a tie clip that I wore for years. From Goodyear Tire & Rubber came a large ash tray in the form of a tire with "EPS Don't Count" imprinted on the metal center. I still have boxes of pencils with the same message from a pencil manufacturer.

But it was an uphill battle and there were many rejections. A salesman is never indifferent to rejection, but you can get inured to it. I learned that as a youngster when I peddled decals to shopkeepers in New York. Free cash flow and the theory of lead steers were certainly harder sells. It was next to impossible to persuade anyone beyond the age of 50. Middle-aged CFOs and CEOs who had lived for years with the conviction that the market could be hoodwinked by manipulating earnings—honest manipulations, to be sure—felt threatened by doctrines that negated everything that they ever knew. Yet I kept calling on them. I could sustain frequent rejection by reminding myself that I had scored some successes.

Some of the rejection was brutal. I remember flying out to Los Angeles to call on the three top executives of Litton Industries, then one of the best known and most successful conglomerates in the United States. Company headquarters were in Beverly Hills, in a building that looked like a private mansion with a circular driveway in front, all of which suggested the headquarters of a movie company. On hand for my presentation were Charles B. Thornton, the CEO; Roy Ash, the COO; and Joe Casey, senior vice president for finance. Casey was the expert on my subject. After I expounded for more than an hour, Thornton and Ash said nothing, and Casey fixed me with his piercing eyes and pronounced a crisp judgment: "I've never heard anybody say what you've said about how the market operates." He did not stop there, repeating with indignation that my views were theoretical musings.

I was utterly deflated and suddenly angry. "Then clearly you've been listening to the wrong people," I snapped. The meeting was a disaster and I was soon on a plane back to New York.

I also called on another celebrated conglomerateur, James Ling of Ling-Temco-Vought. I flew down to Dallas with Allen Marple, head of aerospace lending for Chase, who had set up the meeting. Allen was one of the most gifted and curious minds at Chase and a good friend besides. I made my presentation for two hours. Ling was cordial and seemed receptive; but after I finished, he turned to Marple and said, "May I now present to Joel?" Then he went on for an hour. I have forgotten what he had to say, but it had nothing to do with what I had talked about. It was all an absurd misunderstanding. I thought I was there to sell Ling, and Ling thought he was selling Chase. Meantime, we almost missed our plane; but Ling sent us off in a chauffeured car that rocketed down the highways and then, to my amazement, rolled on to the tarmac and deposited us at the steps of the Braniff plane, which Ling had gotten the airline to wait for us.

Ling was a good friend of Braniff's CEO, Harding Lawrence, whom we found sitting in the first row of the plane. Lawrence also knew Marple, and Lawrence insisted that we sit in the first row and he would move back. We demurred, he insisted, and we finally agreed. I remember Lawrence saying, "Nobody's ever held a plane for me."

Conglomerateurs clearly did not care for my message. I had three sessions with Charles Bluhdorn, who had gained considerable celebrity as a young man for his energetic deal making in putting together Gulf + Western. I thought I had a chance with Bluhdorn, for

I was flattered that he had read one of my articles. At our first meeting, he asked me, "Do you think it pays to smooth earnings?"

I replied, "Not if the market thinks you are smoothing earnings."

He persisted. "Do you therefore think that it pays to fool the market into thinking that I'm not smoothing earnings while I'm doing so?"

I responded by reminding him of the stock observation about one's inability to fool all of the people all of the time.

Bluhdorn's frustration was his sluggish share price, which he felt did not reflect his success in increasing his earnings per share. That success in large part came from acquisitions at too high a price. He was only concerned with covering the interest on the debt he incurred, neglecting the cost of equity capital. I tried to explain the distinction between growth and expansion, as defined in this chapter, but I got nowhere. He was fixated on the EPS goals he had set for his company when speaking to analysts, and I was not helping by talking about what really created value in the eyes of the market. Bluhdorn was more polite than Joe Casey, but he informed me, "I never had anybody come in here to tell me that what I'm doing is wrong."

So there were many disappointments; but by the mid-1970s, my first foreign market opened unexpectedly—South Africa, of all places.

4

A Letter from
Oppenheimer

In 1973, a few months after my articles began to appear in the *Financial Times*, I received a letter from a reader in South Africa asking for further elucidation of some points I had made in a piece on capital structure and risk. The letter was signed "H. Oppenheimer" and was on the letterhead of "La Lucia," which meant nothing to me, nor did the name of the writer (I later learned that La Lucia was a suburb north of Durban). I replied at length, happy to enlighten a distant reader, however unknown. In due course, I received another letter from H. Oppenheimer, this time from Johannesburg and on the letterhead of the Anglo-American Corporation, inviting me to come to South Africa to give a series of lectures at various universities.

I still did not have a clue who Oppenheimer was, but I showed the correspondence to Don Palmer, who ran Chase's Africa and Middle East desk, and asked him what to do. "By all means go," said Palmer, explaining that Oppenheimer was the most prominent businessman in South Africa, head of the De Beers diamond empire and the Anglo-American Corporation, the leading gold mining company, which also controlled scores of industrial corporations. Palmer compared Oppenheimer to David Rockefeller, by which he meant that he had an equally famous family name and presided over enormous assets created by forebears—in Oppenheimer's case by his father, Sir Ernest Oppenheimer.

So I lost no time in accepting the invitation, which opened new worlds to me. It also dramatized a lesson that every salesperson should know: answer every letter that you receive, unless it is obviously wacko. Indeed, my curiosity is such that I can't even resist the impulse to pick up my office phone every time it rings, unless my assistant forestalls me.

I also must confess that after I left Don Palmer's office, I was still confused about precisely where South Africa was; so I consulted a large, illuminated globe at Chase headquarters. In the years since, I've traveled to five of the seven continents and picked up enough geography so as not to be embarrassed. I have not been to Antarctica or South America, and for some reason I have not been south of Mexico, where I had such a memorable visitation of Montezuma's revenge that I vowed never to go there again. (Some years ago, I was invited to talk at a conference of Philip Morris executives in Mexico City. I said that I would accept if I could speak in the morning, so I could arrive the night before, skip dinner and breakfast—the limit of my ability to fast, except religious fasts, of course—and have lunch on the departing plane.)

In Johannesburg, Chase was represented by a small branch, and it also had an equity stake in the Standard and Chartered Bank, a British institution with a large presence in South Africa. The Chase representative at the Standard accompanied me to my first appointment with Oppenheimer at his headquarters in downtown Johannesburg, on Main Street. I was struck by the modesty of Oppenheimer's office, which was matched by the man. He was short and slight, looked to be in his early sixties, and spoke in a soft, barely audible voice—a trait he shared with David Rockefeller. After we

shook hands, I made my standard comment that it was a pleasure finally to put a face to a name, and Oppenheimer replied that he had
long been looking forward to meeting me. He had a warm smile and
a gentle manner, designed to put a visitor at ease. He obviously knew
how intimidating his reputation was likely to be, and he seemed to
go to special lengths to make one feel welcome.

By this time, of course, I knew a great deal about Harry Oppenheimer, for I had done my homework before leaving New York. He
was not only a shrewd and effective businessman, but also a politically independent figure who was often at odds with the Afrikaner
government. He favored promoting blacks to skilled jobs in the
mines and he sought to recognize black labor unions, policies that
were anathema to the regime. Oppenheimer spoke out against
apartheid and he funded opposition politicians. He was too wealthy
and too powerful for the government to squelch.

All of this made me feel comfortable coming to South Africa
under his sponsorship, for I must confess that I had some initial skit-
tishness about visiting a land where racial segregation and discrimination were declared national policy. I could hardly have felt otherwise, for apart from being an American, I was also a member of a
minority, as Oppenheimer was on his father's side. Many South
African Jews, I later discovered, were vocal opponents of apartheid;
the most celebrated was the stalwart Helen Suzman, the lone parlia-
mentary representative of the Progressive party.

At my first meeting with Oppenheimer, he gave me my schedule
and explained that I would be going to Durban and Cape Town, as
well as to many spots around Johannesburg and Pretoria, the administrative capital. I was scheduled to give guest lectures at eight universities—including the universities of Witwatersrand, Cape Town,
and Stellenbosch, the leading Afrikaner university—on the subject
of the revolutionary new developments in the theory of corporate finance, my stock in trade. Oppenheimer also wanted me to meet with
the CEOs of several industrial corporations in the Anglo-American

group. I gathered that he was eager to get their reaction to my heretical views.

On that first visit, I became enamored of South Africa, despite its dismaying social problems. For one thing, the people were so welcoming, whether they were university professors, corporate executives, or my favorite waiter, a young black named Efrem who worked in the Oyster Box Hotel in the town of Umhlanga on the Indian Ocean coast north of Durban. And then there was the sheer physical beauty of the country, a land of immense contrasts—in the central part of the country, miles and miles of grasslands framed in the distance by mountain ranges; on the coast, jagged mountains tumbling down to the sea, interspersed with peaceful coves and pristine beaches.

Cape Town and its environs, on the Atlantic Coast, encapsulate much of the charm and variety of the country. The city itself provides a kaleidoscope of exciting images, from its bustling waterfront at one end to Table Mountain hovering behind the city like a protective shield. In the countryside, no more than an hour's drive from the city, are lush, rolling hills covered with vines and dotted with white stucco wineries. The coastal road south of the city threads its way around cliffs that plunge into the sea, with heart-stopping drops of 500 feet or more, from the circuitous road straight into the water. Further south, at the tip of the continent, is an enormous game preserve; and beyond that, you get magnificent ocean views from a high promontory.

The reaction to my lectures was gratifying, both from faculty members and students. I spent a lot of time, of course, with business types, and it was no surprise that I got a positive reception from executives at the Anglo-American companies. But more than Harry Oppenheimer's sponsorship was involved. South African businesspeople, I discovered, were greatly interested in new ideas. They had enormous curiosity about the outside world, a curiosity nurtured by their geographic isolation, 5,500 miles from Europe. Another factor was the great dependence of the economy on the export trade, which bred a concern for what was happening in foreign lands. As a group, South African business executives also seemed to travel more widely than their U.S. contemporaries. All of which meant a very receptive audience for the message that I brought.

I was impressed with the business success achieved by my hosts, but I was also surprised by their sumptuous wealth, which they took for granted. Their attitude was, "You know, we all live like this, if we've achieved a certain position." This sort of thing is unusual in the United States, where understatement is more often the rule. If a person is a vice president of Merrill Lynch, you don't find him or her living on 8 or 10 acres with a magnificent English Tudor house and a flock of servants. In South Africa, such luxury was no cause for comment.

The first company to retain my services was Tongaat, a sugar producer with vast plantations that became part of the Anglo-American group. Tongaat was located in the town of the same name about 25 miles north of Durban in hot and humid country, much like the U.S. deep South, that was ideal for growing sugar cane. I met Chris Saunders, Tongaat's executive chairman and the son of the founder, during the course of being introduced to several Anglo-American executives. We hit it off, and that first conversation led to a relationship that lasted for more than a decade. Saunders flattered me by wanting a full day of my time three times a year—in November, February, and June. He was fascinated by what was going on in the United States, but his interest was more than academic. At that time, South Africa was a commodity supplier to the West—this was long before the era of sanctions—and so Saunders felt that a large part of his country's near-term performance was dependent on the health of the U.S. economy.

My visits to Tongaat soon fell into a pattern. In the morning, I would meet with Ted Garner, the company's chief financial officer, and his staff. I would give them an overview of the U.S. economy, discussing developments since my last visit, then zero in on Tongaat's own situation. I would review my valuation analysis of the company, piece by piece, aggregated to look at the company's total valuation, and then compare it with Tongaat's peer group of companies. We would spend some time looking at their acquisition strategy and analyzing their capital structure—the mix of debt and equity—and any financing plans they had for the future.

By then it was time for lunch, and we would repair to Saunders's former home, which was nearby. He had grown up in this palatial house—a masterpiece of white stucco Cape Dutch architecture, with floors made of ancient tiles covered with oriental and African rugs. Saunders and his managing director, Alan Hankinson, would join Garner and myself, and I would fill them in on what was going on in the United States, politically and economically. There was a lot to talk about, for it was a turbulent time in U.S. affairs, what with the Watergate scandal, Nixon's forced resignation, the government's efforts to grapple with the country's inflationary surge, the close election of 1976 between Ford and Carter (there was a lot of curiosity about the "peanut farmer"), and much else, as the years rolled on.

After a capacious lunch, Alan Hankinson would put me in his Mercedes, and we would drive for miles around the plantation until he found an appropriate shady spot, where he would park and throw open the doors. Then for hours we would discuss corporate strategy. Why didn't we do this in an air-conditioned office? He wanted privacy and he didn't want to be interrupted.

What I had to say was apparently of some use to them, and it was certainly a pleasure for me to have such an attentive audience in such an exotic place. What I contributed essentially was to instruct them in how to be a successful conglomerate (they were expanding into building materials and clothing), which essentially meant not paying too much for acquisitions. They were proceeding largely by intuition; I provided the technical analytic framework that allowed them to fine-tune their efforts. It did not cost Tongaat much, I think about $10,000 a year; but the company also paid my airfare, so I was able to seek other clients at the same time, at little expense to my employer.

My second South African client came on the recommendation of Tongaat. Chris Saunders introduced me to Dr. Kees van der Pol, the CEO of a company called Huletts, another sugar producer. At first glance, this might seem odd, something like Ford introducing a consultant to GM; but the two companies were not really competitors, for they both sold a commodity, not a brand, and they jointly used the same sugar mills. In the end Tongaat and Huletts merged; but before that happened, I had Huletts as a client for a few years. That connection also led to a third client, in the daisy-chain manner in which these things often work. On Huletts's board was a Scot named Jack Ward, the chief executive of Romatex, a textile and carpet manufacturer located in Durban proper. Ward was sufficiently impressed with the work I was doing for Huletts to hire me to provide the same counsel for Romatex. Jack's firm was largely owned by a conglomerate; but he was as much of an entrepreneur as any I have known, intuitively grasping all aspects of the valuation approach and its application to strategic planning. Our business friendship was one I had hoped would last the rest of my career; but unfortunately Jack was a generation older than I was, and he retired about seven years later.

So I now had three clients on the Natal coast, close to each other, which meant that the revenue was getting interesting. At the time, I introduced a principle that has been ironclad ever since: transportation and hotel expenses were shared among nearby clients. No multiple billing.

My fourth client was considerably larger—an Anglo-American entity called South African Breweries, one of the largest industrial companies in the country that produces 98 percent of the beer consumed in South Africa. Not long afterward, I met Dr. Anton Rupert, the leading Afrikaner businessman—widely regarded as the Afrikaner counterpart of Harry Oppenheimer—who headed the Rembrandt group. Rupert hired Chase for several assignments. Once we had Rembrandt as well as Anglo-American, we felt we had arrived.

My trips to South Africa were by no means devoted solely to bringing the new financial enlightenment to receptive businessmen. After my guest lecture at the University of Cape Town during my first visit, Meyer Feldberg, the dean of the university's Graduate School of Business, asked me to return the following year to give a full course in his MBA program on new developments in financial theory. I readily accepted. My schedule did not allow for the normal leisurely pace of an academic course, with two or three one-hour sessions a week for a quarter or a semester. Instead, either I gave the course during two visits (each of which lasted about a fortnight), or I lectured for three hours a day, five days a week, for two weeks running—a total of 30 hours.

Offhand, this would seem to be an enormous burden on the lecturer, but I thrived on it. After all, I had a lot of experience with those management seminars back home, which involved nonstop talking for two days, seven hours a day. Not for nothing was I called "Marathon Joel" when I was introduced to a new class. I did tell the students, however, that if I fell asleep before they did, they would be excused from the rest of the lecture. That never happened, but I suffered from recurrent nightmares in which I was compelled to lecture continuously for 30 hours, from 9 A.M. Monday to 3 P.M. Tuesday, with the students given a midterm exam at midnight Monday and the final exam Tuesday afternoon.

I taught at Cape Town for eight years. Early on, I met Brian Kantor, a brilliant professor of economics at the university, and his talented and beautiful artist wife, Shirley, together with their two sons, Charles and Daniel. Brian and Shirley are charming and delightful companions and we became close friends, seeing each other regularly for nigh on to 25 years. Despite my enjoyment of Cape Town, in 1985 I accepted an invitation to switch my course to Witwater-srand University in Johannesburg. I had found that there was not enough business in Cape Town to warrant the time I was spending there, whereas there was a lot more activity in Joburg: business meetings from breakfast until 4 P.M., then classes from 5 P.M. to 9 P.M.—no extra days needed.

I learned a lot in South Africa, but not only from businessmen and academic types. I've mentioned Efrem, my favorite waiter at the Oyster Box Hotel. We became friendly because Efrem discovered that I was inordinately fond of the fish cakes served at the hotel. Whenever I appeared for Sunday breakfast, Efrem made sure that fish cakes were available.

One November, I said that I looked forward to seeing him the following February. "I won't be here," said Efrem, "I'll be on holiday for three weeks." I inquired where he was off to, and he said he was going back to Mozambique, his homeland, to see his wife and children. He explained that the Mozambique government did not allow families to accompany workers like himself who went abroad for jobs. He was in South Africa because the pay was enormously better than it was at home; poor as conditions were for blacks in South Africa, they were still considerably better than in most nearby lands. In effect, Efrem was willing to go into exile in order to support his family, even though the Mozambique government confiscated much of his earnings (paid in gold) when he returned home. It amounted to the government holding his family as hostages. Efrem suggested that if economic conditions were better elsewhere in southern Africa, the immigration flow would run in the reverse direction, with South Africans exporting themselves to escape apartheid, which of course did not exist elsewhere. A large enough exodus would inevitably undermine apartheid in South Africa, for the economy was dependent on a large supply of relatively cheap black labor, relative to what white workers earned. This was a pipe dream, of course, because these other countries were governed at the time by politicians bedazzled by Marxist socialist nostrums. But it was quite an insight, first imparted to me by an untutored waiter.

In 1976, Harry Oppenheimer proposed that my family accompany me on my summer visit. So Karen, Erik (almost five), and I toured the country and saw a lot of the Kruger National Park, the vast wild game preserve where Karen spotted her first "tiger," only to be told by the guide that there were none in South Africa. In 1976 as well, to my surprise, I found myself regarded as something of an expert on the country. At least that was the view of the Subcommittee on African Affairs of the Senate Foreign Relations Committee, which invited me to testify on economic conditions in South Africa. I did so on September 9, 1976. I sought to explain why the country suffered from high inflation and a large balance-of-payments deficit after enjoying years of stability and high growth in the 1960s. I located the problem in the huge increase in the money supply after the gold standard was abandoned internationally in 1971. The result was a massive surge in the price of gold and a substantial rise in South Africa's export revenue, for gold was one of its major exports.

In my view, the government at that time made "two principal errors." The first was its refusal to let the rand float sufficiently upward, instead holding it to the fixed rate of $1.40. Then, after a predictable buildup in the country's balance-of-payment-surplus and its foreign-exchange reserves, causing the money supply to explode and the inflation rate to soar, the government erred again by refusing for the longest time to clamp down with deflationary measures. Devaluation of the rand finally came in September 1975. (My colleagues and I had estimated that had the government permitted the rand to reach $1.60, inflation over the past 25 years would have been mild, if not downright tame.)

In the late 1980s, I got caught up in the argument about economic sanctions against South Africa. The goal was to pressure the Afrikaner government to end apartheid. I certainly favored the goal; but I was opposed to the trade embargo on the grounds that it would lead to international black markets and higher prices and, more important, that it would hurt the bottom half of the population to the extent to which it was effective. Many would lose their jobs. And in the end they did.

At one point, I engaged in a long distance debate about sanctions on NBC's "Today" show with the late Reverend Leon Sullivan, then well-known for the "Sullivan principles," which he formulated to guide the employment practices of U.S. corporations in South Africa. (Among other things, they had to guarantee no discrimination in hiring and promotion practices, and they had to grant the right of collective bargaining.) Bryant Gumbel, the host at that time, had Sullivan speak first. He made an eloquent case for sanctions, while I was shaking my head in the London NBC studio. When my turn came, I made my argument about the dismal effect sanctions would have on the poor. Sullivan responded heatedly, and I added to the decibel count, with the argument getting personal. I suggested that he sat comfortably in Philadelphia while asking his African brothers and sisters to take it on the chin.

Looking back, I've changed my mind. Sullivan was right and I was wrong. Sanctions helped end apartheid, for they made the whole world aware of the problem and they made the Afrikaner government realize they were pariahs. The apartheid laws were first softened and then ended. In February 1990, Nelson Mandela was released from prison after an incarceration of 27 years. He surprised the world by disavowing any interest in retribution and instead promoted racial reconciliation and cooperation with the white power structure. He has truly been a heroic figure, perhaps as great as Gandhi, though their methods differed, to put it mildly. History will also applaud the wisdom of President F. W. de Klerk, who negotiated with Mandela and ended the long nightmare of apartheid.

These days, of course, South Africa has other economic and social problems. The enfranchisement of the entire population and the election of Mandela as state president in 1994 led to buoyant (and perhaps unachievable) expectations of economic growth and a rising standard of living that have not been fulfilled. Unemployment is high; the government's housing program has fallen far short of its goals; and the value of the country's currency, the rand, has fallen dramatically on the foreign exchange markets.

Economic growth has simply been inadequate to fulfill the hopes of a liberated population. There are many reasons for this failure. One problem is the tax system, with its negative incentives. Marginal tax rates are simply too high. Anyone earning the equivalent of $15,000 to $20,000 reaches the 30 percent tax bracket. Even more important is inadequate foreign investment to spur the level of growth needed, for there is just not enough domestic capital to do the job. The shortfall in foreign investment, in turn, has been a prime cause of the decline of the rand.

Foreign capital is skittish for several reasons. First of all, there is the question of personal security. The high crime rate is a deterrent to many business visitors and undermines confidence in long-range investment schemes. The Mbeki government, like the Mandela government before it, has been incapable of dealing adequately with urban crime. Too few criminals are arrested; and of those arrested, too many are released too soon. A major problem has been the quality of the police force, trained to repress dissent under the Afrikaner government and not adequately trained to repress crime.

Second, foreigners are aware that there are still significant restrictions on capital flows for South African residents, although they have been relaxed somewhat. These restrictions do not apply to foreign-owned capital; but there is understandable fear that at some point in the future similar restrictions could be applied to foreigners, who might then be unable to get their money out of the country.

Third, there is what might be called political risk. The push for black ownership in the name of "empowerment," though mild today, raises anxieties about expropriation sometime in the future. Some of the atmospherics of the Mbeki government are unsettling, such as its initial unwillingness to condemn the rigged election of Robert Mugabe in Zimbabwe in March 2002. (Mbeki later shifted course and voted to suspend Zimbabwe from the Commonwealth for a year.) More important has been the failure of the South African government to grapple effectively with the AIDS crisis, even questioning the well-established causal relationship between HIV and AIDS.

But I have never given up on South Africa, which has the human talent and the natural resources to do great things. Our Johannesburg office, established in 1995, was Stern Stewart's first foreign outpost. We have numbered among our clients such prominent firms as the ABSA bank; the JD Group, a nationwide chain of furniture and electronic stores; the New Clicks retail chain of cosmetics and drugstores; Telkom, the state-owned telecommunications company; and the Premier Group.

I continue to go to South Africa at least three times a year, to lecture and to visit clients and potential clients. I am building a year-round house in one of the most agreeable suburbs of Cape Town, of which more later. When the Christmas holidays approach in New York, I fly south. In addition, I spend six weeks there in our summer, teaching at the business school of the University of Cape Town, where I have been appointed a visiting professor.

South Africa's long-term future remains bright, so one remains tolerant of occasional inconveniences. One such episode befell me a few years ago. I was taking a prospective employee to dinner at a restaurant in Sandton, a suburb of Johannesburg. When we arrived at the parking lot, I was impressed with how good the service was, for both doors were opened simultaneously. But before I got out, I found a revolver pressed into my side. It took little urging for me to surrender my wallet and my watch (fortunately, my passport was back at the hotel). Meantime, my companion was relieved of her handbag and her car. A bit shaken, we then entered the restaurant to summon the police. After expressing his regrets, the restaurant owner asked,

"Are you still interested in dinner?" I was still hungry enough for dinner, but I pointed out that I now had no cash and no credit cards.

"Then perhaps you are no longer interested in dinner," said the restaurateur.

I dined out on that comment for weeks. But it was one of the few unkind things ever said to me in South Africa.

5

On Our Own

The "Stern gang" was the label applied to us by the *New York Post* in its November 9, 1982, article about our departure from the Chase Manhattan Bank to create the new firm of Stern Stewart Putnam & Macklis. I did not appreciate the label, with its echo of the Zionist terrorist group that harried the British prior to the creation of the state of Israel in 1948. And, besides, who likes to be called a gang leader? But the *Post* was accurate—the term was bandied about at the time—and I certainly was grateful for the free publicity. Every bit of attention was welcome.

As the sequence of names in the firm name indicates, from the outset, I was managing partner and G. Bennett Stewart III was my number two, later being named senior partner. I had hired Bennett shortly after he graduated from the University of Chicago in 1976, and he quickly fulfilled my expectations in his work at Chase Financial Policy. From the outset, he showed a firm grasp of the theoretical material, he was as practical as he was intellectually deft, and his ebullient personality quickly won friends—and converts to our approach. He turned out to be a great salesman.

Bennett tells an amusing story of his job interview with me. I invited him to breakfast at Ratner's restaurant on the lower East Side, together with Dennis Soter, a close associate of mine at Chase (who later joined Stern Stewart, a decade after its founding). Ratner's was a celebrated and venerable Jewish dairy restaurant, not the sort of place Bennett frequented, but it was a favorite of mine. Despite the early hour, I was soon in full flood of exposition; and, as Bennett tells the story, I was totally unconcerned when the scrambled eggs served by the waiter landed in my lap. I simply lifted my napkin and redeposited the eggs on my plate. (Bennett did not know enough Yiddish to realize that this made the waiter a schlemiel and me a schlomozzle, according to the ancient definitions.) After breakfast, the three of us got into my car, which I suddenly decided needed washing. So we went to a car wash and, rather than interrupt the conversation, sat through the torrents of water and the huge brushes rolling over us, all the while talking financial theory. Fortunately the car had no leaks.

Of the other partners in the original firm title, Bluford H. Putnam III had been one of the senior economists at Chase and was a well-known figure in the field. After two years with us, he left to become chief international economist at Morgan Stanley. Jeffrey Macklis was a talented software specialist who designed a software program that embraced our value-based management system. We made it available on a mainframe computer and sold access to companies for an annual fee. (This was before PCs became ubiquitous.) Macklis also departed after a couple of years for broader horizons.

Of the five other partners who came from Chase, David Glassman and Donald H. Chew have stayed the course. (The other three who left at various points were E. Mark Gressle, Gordon A. Jensen, and Jay Hayman.) Glassman, whom I hired at Chase back in 1979, has held a variety of important posts and is currently the U.S. partner, in charge of quality control, in our China offices. He took up the post without any knowledge of Chinese but with vast erudition in what might be called financial engineering; no one knows more about the mechanics of EVA implementation. He has handled some of the most difficult EVA assignments that we have undertaken.

Don Chew, then as now, edits Stern Stewart's quarterly journal. A man with a deft editorial pencil, Chew was especially qualified for the job, for he has a Ph.D. in English as well as an MBA, both from the University of Rochester. The journal first made its debut in the fall of 1981 when we were at Chase and was called the *Chase Financial Quarterly* (CFQ). It was my idea and resulted from my realization that businesspeople, even those with a marked intellectual bent, simply did not keep up with the latest academic advances in economics and finance. None that I knew read the academic journals, not because of a lack of interest but because of the inaccessibility of scholarly articles. They were full of language that was either cryptic or turgid, often both, and relied heavily on statistical arrays and complex equations. Moreover, the authors of these articles assumed that readers had already mastered prior articles on the same subject; there was always a bibliography. Readers who could not handle econometrics were at a complete loss.

So my idea was to publish a journal that presented the latest academic research in plain English. An editor's note in the first issue stated that "the articles in *CFQ* will attempt to preserve the intellectual rigor and the analytical quality of the research, while simplifying refinements of theory and statistical technique." My passion for enlightening the business community was not entirely disinterested, of course. I was always on the lookout for ways to distinguish the services of Chase from those of our rivals—to establish brand identity. No other commercial bank was putting out anything like the publication I had in mind, which seemed reason enough to do it.

It proved easier to finance than I had anticipated. I peddled subscriptions, but not with a mass mailing and not for a pittance. I called on businesspeople whom I knew and proposed that each buy a year's subscription for $5,000. We needed this unusually large amount because circulation was likely to be limited to, at best, several hundred readers. I sold 30 subscriptions; $150,000 was enough to launch. Among the articles in the first issue were "The Evidence against Stock Splits" (they don't raise share prices, except to the extent that they signal future improved performance by the firm), "Is Deep Discount Debt Financing a Bargain?" (only the tax treatment is helpful), and "Deflating Inflation Accounting" (investors seem to be indifferent to it).

When our group left Chase, we were allowed to take the journal with us. "We are not in the publishing business," said Bob Lichten, with whom I had that crucial interview, when asked about the fate of the journal. It proved to be a substantial asset, then and in the future. We were resolved to keep our expenses down—we paid ourselves very little—and we were able to use the journal to barter for rent. Harry Abplanalp, my old friend from Chase, was then running the U.S. operations of the Midland Bank, one of Britain's five leading banks. Midland had some spare office space on Lexington Avenue and so Harry agreed to give us free rent in exchange for the journal, which was then renamed the *Midland Corporate Financial Journal*. The publication retained the Midland name until 1987, after which it was renamed the *Journal of Applied Corporate Finance* and was successively sponsored by the Continental Bank and, in 1995, by the Bank of America after it acquired Continental. In 2002, Accenture became co-publisher of the *Journal* with Stern Stewart.

Our rent-free quarters were modest—a mere 3,000 square feet, a low-ceilinged cluster of small offices and a bull pen, into which we squeezed nine partners and just one secretary. It was sometime before we felt we could afford another secretary. But our spirits were high. It was exhilarating to be on our own. Our financial backer, Ron Palamara, did not interfere; but he did put a representative of his company, Anacomp, on our board. At our first board meeting, Anacomp's man asked what our business plan was for the year. I was a bit startled. It had not occurred to me to draw up a formal plan, but I quickly replied, "Our business plan for the year is to have revenues of $4 million and profits of $2 million."

"There's no way in the world that you can deliver those results," the Anacomp rep said scornfully. I did not argue; but to avoid further questioning, I called no more board meetings. In the end, our first year's profit came to $2.2 million—an indication of how lucrative consulting can be, especially if salaries are kept artificially low. David Glassman, for one, complained that we were so profitable because we paid ourselves such meager salaries. He had a point. And we couldn't pay bonuses out of profits because we wanted to buy out Anacomp as soon as possible. There was reason for this sense of urgency. Ron Palamara, our benefactor, discovered he had advanced stomach cancer only months after we opened our doors. Anacomp was doing badly, and we feared it might go bankrupt. If that happened, the Chase Manhattan Bank, a large lender to Anacomp, might gain control of the company and thus end up owning 50 percent of our firm. As mentioned in Chapter 1, we succeeded in buying out Anacomp after two years. Out of gratitude and respect for Ron, I added $250,000 to the $5 million he had put up so that he could report a profit on his investment in our firm.

At the new firm, we continued the kind of advisory work that we had undertaken at Chase, but we added some new ventures. One was Jeffrey Macklis's software program, which enabled clients to calculate effortlessly their cost of capital, NOPAT (net operating profit after tax), the present value of future cash flows, and so on.

Another new venture was a monthly newsletter, *Stern Advice*, which we launched with a full-page ad in *Barron's*. "JOEL STERN GOES PUBLIC," the ad proclaimed in large type, with *Stern Advice* described as the first newsletter that "dares to share the real inside story" of what goes on in the nation's corporate boardrooms. It would be more than a stock tip sheet, and it would deal with the "difficult issues," the "big picture." For all this, the reader was asked to pay $250 for a year's subscription. *Stern Advice* was edited by our economist, Bluford Putnam, and consisted of analytic pieces by him, myself, and others; market commentary; a list of 10 recommended stocks of the month; and, from time to time (whenever I returned from South Africa), forecasts of the price of gold. My South African contacts presumably endowed me with expertise in this area, but I would not try it again. Unhappily, the newsletter only lasted a year. Joel Stern's advice was to shut down *Stern Advice*, with much encouragement from my partners. We lacked the capital to promote it adequately. It cost two dollars in advertising to generate one dollar in subscription revenue. It takes years for many newsletters to escape this losing relationship.

Far more successful were the training programs that we launched. The senior management seminars had won us a following, and we found ready acceptance for our new offerings. One was a five-day training program in financial theory and practice for the finance departments of commercial banks and accounting firms. Another was a three-day course for bank executives on corporate restructuring, an especially popular offering during the leveraged-buyout frenzy of the 1980s. It was lucrative work. For the five-day course, for example, we charged a $10,000–$14,000 fee for each day. One year we ran 35 training programs all over the country, with Bennett and myself doing most of the lecturing. We managed to arrange the schedules of our personal appearances so that we could run both a five-day program and a three-day program in the same city at the same time. At its peak, this activity accounted for 60 percent or more of the firm's revenues. These programs also broadcast our corporate identity to an average of 30 people at each session. Many of these people would subsequently leave their firms and become buyers of our services elsewhere.

Toward the end of the 1980s, we fully developed the concept of Economic Value Added, which eventually became the emblem and principal product of Stern Stewart. It was a gradual evolution. As discussed in Chapter 3, for years I had been decrying the distortions inherent in using accounting measures to determine the value of a company, a property, or a project. The most accurate method, I eventually argued, was to use a discounted free-cash-flow analysis, using the cost of capital as the discount rate. (Inherent in the cost of capital is the relevant risk factor, which every sophisticated investor takes into consideration—hence its importance in the calculation.) Discounting future free cash flows to present value thus allows a comparison with a company's share price or with the cost of a new acquisition or project. The green light flashes if the cost is below the present value of projected free cash flows.

So for a long time (since 1972, when the model was properly designed), we had been using free cash flow in our corporate advisory work—and gaining scores of converts. And we were not alone. The methodology gained widespread acceptance as the years passed and the Miller-Modigliani theses conquered the academic world and spread beyond it. But one calculation that free cash did not provide was a contemporaneous, period-by-period measure of corporate performance. It would, of course, have been possible to calculate a firm's present value (PV) of projected free cash flows in year one, repeat the process in year two, and compare the two PVs. But there was an obvious drawback to such an effort. One would be comparing projections, not actual results. And projections were necessarily "iffy" and could also be manipulated by a management unscrupulous about showing improvement.

So the search was on in our shop for what came to be known as Economic Value Added. (Bennett Stewart remembers my using that term occasionally in the 1970s to characterize the free cash flow from new investment that exceeded the dollar amount of the investment.) We had many conversations about the matter, in which Bennett made a substantial contribution; and what finally emerged was a rock solid calculation of a firm's economic performance—as distinguished from its accounting performance—from one period to the next.

Simply put, EVA is the profit that results after deducting the cost of all the capital invested in the firm (equity as well as debt). We start with NOPAT, from which we deduct a capital charge. That charge is calculated by multiplying the cost of capital by the amount of capital employed. For example, if a company's cost of capital is 12 percent and the amount of capital is $10,000, the capital charge is $1,200. If NOPAT is $3,000, the sum of $1,200 is deducted, and the result is an EVA of $1,800. (If NOPAT is less than the capital charge, EVA is a negative number.) It is then easy to compare a firm's EVA in year one with that in year two, and so on. Of course, the comparison can also be made if the EVA figures are negative; less negative EVA in year two obviously shows improvement.

We had been using all the ingredients in the new equation for some time. For example, we had long been calculating the weighted average cost of capital (both equity and debt capital), as described in Chapter 3. This led to dramatically different results from the accounting method, which only considered the cost of debt capital. And we had long been adjusting NOPAT to eliminate accounting distortions and to get down to a true operating profit. As John S. Shiely and I wrote about NOPAT in our 2001 book, *The EVA Challenge*:

> At first glance, the term may sound redundant, for *net* normally means "after tax." Here net refers to adjustments to eliminate various accounting distortions. If we simply used the accountants' bottom line, NOPAT would [in almost all instances] understate true economic profit, for accounting rules treat as current expenses too many items that, from a shareholder's standpoint, should properly be on the balance sheet as assets. The staff at Stern Stewart have found over 120 accounting "anomalies," as they are politely called, but most companies require no more than a dozen adjustments to make their NOPATs realistic. . . .

Among the most common adjustments [are] (1) research-and-development (R&D) costs, (2) advertising and promotion, and (3) staff training and development. Accountants expense R&D, presumably because these outlays would be worth nothing if the firm went belly-up. That consideration is undoubtedly of interest to lenders concerned with liquidation value, but it is totally unrealistic in calculating the true profitability of a company. R&D is properly considered an investment that will bring future returns. Under EVA, it is included in the company's balance sheet and is amortized over the period of years during which these research outlays are expected to have an impact. Only the yearly amortization charge is included as a cost item in deriving NOPAT.

Similarly, under EVA accounting, the part of advertising that is undertaken for a long-term purpose, such as to establish brand identity, is treated the same way as R&D. The same logic holds for staff training and development, whose results are expected to persist for years as an investment that improves the value of the firm's human capital. As for taxes, only actual payments during the year show up in the NOPAT calculations; reserves for deferred taxes are excluded. There are other adjustments as well to eliminate accounting distortions and to present the economic reality of the firm. So we had all the components of EVA in our shop. The breakthrough came when we put them together.

Thus, EVA should be seen as a device to perform zero-based budgeting as an ongoing exercise. This means reviewing all assets to determine if they should be expanded or contracted, retained or sold, as if the investment decisions were being made now for the first time. This is the kind of corporate culture that leads management to take decisions in a timely fashion, with plans being updated continuously instead of at a prescribed annual planning meeting.

EVA became of great utility not only as a measure of performance but also as a total management system that includes incentives. As a management system, EVA became a guide to where value can be created in the firm, for the performance measure is not limited to the company as a whole. EVA can also be calculated for each corporate division, business unit, factory, store, and even product line, so long as the relevant data are available—operating results, amount of capital employed, and cost of capital. And the reporting period does not have to be limited to a year; results can be churned out monthly, even weekly.

This flexibility enables management to identify trouble spots and to determine where to expand, where to retrench, where to economize on the use of capital, where to invest more capital. EVA is a useful tool as well to appraise proposed acquisitions or divestitures. In this regard, while it produces the same results as discounted free-cash-flow analysis, EVA does more than produce a present value figure. Its projections also indicate the future years in which EVA becomes positive.

These nuanced applications were not apparent when we first formulated the EVA concept; they developed gradually as we implemented EVA for different clients. From the outset, however, we sold EVA as an incentive system. With a solid period-to-period performance measure, it was relatively easy to link incentive pay to actual achievement—and to set performance targets three years in advance. We will discuss the details in a later chapter on incentives, which will also describe the novel incentive plan that we devised for Stern Stewart.

While a rising EVA indicates that true economic profit and thus shareholder value are increasing, an allied measure called Market Value Added (MVA) captures the overall gain more precisely than EVA does. MVA, another concept created by Stern Stewart around the same time as EVA, measures the difference in any period between the market value of a company—its market capitalization—and the amount of capital that investors and lenders have funneled into the company over the years. The capital figure includes the book value of debt and equity, including retained earnings. The total investment since day one is then compared with market value. It is a simple comparison: cash in, cash out. If the market cap is greater than the total invested, MVA is positive. Investors can take out more cash than they put in. If the MVA is negative, wealth has been destroyed.

As Shiely and I wrote in *The EVA Challenge*:

> There is a significant link between MVA growth and growth in EVA. Rising EVA tends to foreshadow increases in MVA, though there is no one-to-one correlation. . . . Put another way, the basic theory is that MVA is the present value of [all expected] future EVA. If expectations turn out to be unrealistic, then it could be argued that the present-day price was too high or too low. But the key point is that [MVA is fundamentally driven by EVA, and thus there is no surprise that] there is a very strong correlation between changes in MVA and changes in EVA. In fact, the correlation is three times better than the correlation between changes in MVA and earnings per share or cash flow, and twice as good as the correlation with return on equity.

While we had boundless confidence in our unique product, EVA did not get off to a swift start, for the concept was new and companies needed a fair amount of persuasion to try it. The cause got a big boost in 1991 with the publication of Bennett Stewart's massive volume, *The Quest for Value*. The book eloquently demolished the "market myths" that had long bedazzled investors and security analysts, effectively elaborating on themes that I had advanced in my articles and seminars in the 1970s and especially in my book *Analytical Methods in Financial Planning* (1974).

Bennett's book made the case strongly for EVA. *The Quest for Value* became the EVA bible, which we distributed to anyone who evinced an interest in the subject but which, I fear, like the bible, was rarely read cover to cover. It is 781 pages long and could crack your ribs if you tried to read it in bed. We insiders humorously refer to it as *The Neverending Quest for Value*. It is still in print and still selling. In 1998, it was supplemented by a more accessible and highly readable book by my partner Al Ehrbar.

Despite the debut of EVA, the period 1990–1991 was a difficult one at Stern Stewart. Our training business fell off sharply, due to the end of the leveraged-buyout frenzy and thus the interest of banks and accounting firms in the niceties of valuation techniques and financial theory. At the same time, our consulting work declined largely because we charged fees, whereas investment banks were offering similar advisory services gratis. They made their money from underwriting fees, trading for their own account and brokerage fees.

It was a tough time. There was no money for bonuses, the partners paid themselves very little, and at times we wondered if we could meet our annual payroll of $1.5 million. If we went under, my own liability amounted to about $1 million, for I then owned 50 percent of the firm. Two colleagues resigned their partnerships and stayed on as employees. Given the prospect of personal liability, it seemed a prudent move to them then—but not later, when we revived.

We had completed about two dozen EVA implementations when *Fortune* magazine, in its September 20, 1993, issue came out with a cover proclaiming, "The Real Key to Creating Wealth—It's Called EVA." The seven-page article, by Shawn Tully, eloquently highlighted the virtues of EVA: "What if you could look at almost any business operation and see immediately whether it was becoming more valuable or less? What if you as a manager could use this measure to make sure your operation—however large or small—was increasing in value? What if you as an investor could use it to spot stocks that were far likelier than most to rise high?"

Although there were other consultants in the field, Tully wrote,

"The preeminent popularizer of the concept is Stern Stewart & Co. of New York City, which calls it economic value added, or EVA. It is today's hottest financial idea and getting hotter." A better journalistic send-off could hardly have been imagined. The article described the mechanics of computing EVA, printed a box on "Ways to Raise EVA," presented the case for an EVA-based incentive system, and discussed how EVA was used to great advantage by Quaker Oats and Briggs & Stratton, two of four clients of ours who were mentioned. As a result of their success with EVA, both Quaker Oats and Briggs & Stratton had been rewarded with substantial run-ups in their share prices. The article even ran a picture of Bennett and me, brooding over a chess board.

The *Fortune* article was one of those publicity breaks in the hope of which public relations firms extract large fees from their clients. Not so in our case; it was all serendipitous, although it can be regarded as the fruit of our regular effort to be visible in the marketplace of ideas. In April 1993, we had held what we called the "Stern Stewart Roundtable on Relationship Investing and Shareholder Communications." Attending were businesspeople and academics and one journalist, Geoffrey Colvin, an editor of *Fortune*. During the exchanges, EVA came in for some mention. Colvin found the concept intriguing, and at one point he remarked that he thought it was the sort of innovation that his magazine should write about. Five months later the article appeared.

The *Fortune* piece transformed our business lives. We were deluged with inquiries from at home and abroad. We were a small shop with about 20 professionals, and we had to hire and train new staff to go out into the field to install EVA programs. And the results? In the fourth quarter of 1993, our revenues more than equalled those of the first three quarters. We were on our way.

6

How We Grew

In 1993, Stern Stewart was retained by Fletcher Challenge, the largest industrial group in New Zealand, to install an EVA program. My willingness to go anywhere, at any time, landed the assignment. Almost 20 years before, I had done some work for Sir Ronald Trotter when he was CEO of Challenge Corporation, before its merger with Fletcher, after which he became chairman of the new company. I had renewed contact with Sir Ronald after seeing him by chance on a TV travelogue about New Zealand. I filled him in on EVA, which interested him greatly, and I finally proposed to fly to New Zealand to present the program to his board of directors. Sir Ronald told me that there was no prospect of success, for the board was about to hire a rival consulting company at the urging of Hugh Fletcher, the company's CEO. But I persisted. I told him that I was eager to present my ideas if he was willing to pay my round-trip airfare. He agreed.

After arriving in New Zealand, I made presentations on a Friday to the firm's executive committee, on Sunday to its strategic planning committee, and on Monday to the board. It was all a bit exhausting, but it had a happy pay-off. On Tuesday, Sir Ronald told me that we were hired. I soon learned that the board members switched to us because they were impressed (quite apart from the merits of my presentation) by my willingness to undertake the long trip from New York on the chance of making a sale. In my enthusiasm, I also pledged to return every six weeks to attend sessions of the steering committee that they would be setting up to oversee the EVA implementation.

All went well for a time. I attended a couple of steering committee meetings. Then one afternoon, shortly before I was to leave my New York office for the airport, my assistant informed me that she had failed to renew my visa. It took four days to get one from the New Zealand consulate. What to do? I had Sir Ronald's mobile phone number and swiftly calculated that, given the time difference, I could reach him at home early in the morning.

He was on his morning canter when I called, and I heard a loud "Whoa!" after I announced my name. I explained what had happened and apologized for having to cancel the trip. "That's no problem!" Sir Ronald bellowed. He was a big man, well over six feet tall, built like a rugby player; and he had a hearty laugh that made you feel terrific. "That's no problem!" he repeated, and he outlined a plan of action. I should fly out as scheduled—American Airlines to Los Angeles, then Air New Zealand to Auckland. At each ticket counter, when asked to show my visa, I should offer to sign a document guaranteeing that I would pay the return fare if I was not admitted to New Zealand. Then, when I arrived in Auckland, I should tell the immigration agent that I did not need a visa because I was a missionary. I was incredulous, but Sir Ronald insisted that the ploy would work. "Look him in the eye," he urged. "Be emphatic."

I followed his instructions to the letter. I had no problem at New York's Kennedy Airport or in Los Angeles, and when I arrived at the airport in Auckland, I marched up to the first immigration clerk who was free and presented my passport. He flipped through it and finally said, "There's no visa here." And I stood there, looked him in the eye, and said, very proudly, "I don't need a visa. I'm a missionary." He said, "I never heard of that before." Startled, I put one foot behind the other, made a military pivot, and started walking back in the direction of the plane, whereupon he said, "Excuse me. Where do you think you're going?"

"I can't get into New Zealand," I replied. "I might as well go back to the airplane and fly back to the United States."

"Get back here," he ordered. And so I swiveled around again and returned to his desk.

And he said, "Sir Ronald told us you would say that. We're going to give you a three-day stamp. You can stay in the country for three days and then we want you to get the hell out of here." And that's how I got to attend the steering committee meeting.

At Stern Stewart, we thought of ourselves as missionaries, promoting the cause of financial integrity by selling the EVA brand. When we started publishing a house organ, we called it the *EVAngelist*, which caused some people to smile. But more took us seriously. And business rolled in. Starting in 1994, our revenues doubled each year for two years and kept growing substantially. When the original *Fortune* article had appeared, we were a boutique shop with 20 professionals, as I mentioned before. We had but one office, in New York. We serviced our foreign clients by flying staff out of New York. Greg Milano made so many trips in one year—to Australia, New Zealand, and 33 to Europe alone—that United Airlines named a jumbo jet after him. By the turn of the century, we had offices as far away as Melbourne and Singapore and employed some 200 professionals.

The momentum that came from the 1993 *Fortune* article continued for some time and was renewed annually by another article in the magazine, which came out each autumn or early winter, that featured our Performance 1,000 rankings. The first such list had appeared in Bennett Stewart's 1991 book, *The Quest for Value*. Once the list was published annually, it became probably the single best promotional tool that we had. It presented the Market Value Added performance of the thousand largest U.S. nonfinancial corporations, size being determined by market capitalization. The MVA ranking, from 1 to 1,000, was in turn determined by the dollar value of each company's Market Value Added at the end of the prior year. (We explained the MVA calculation in detail in the last chapter.) Thus by glancing over the list, a reader could determine the extent to which any of the thousand companies had increased—or destroyed—shareholder wealth.

The top wealth creators, year after year, were such well-run corporations as General Electric, Wal-Mart, Merck, Intel, Microsoft, Philip Morris, Exxon, Pfizer, and Procter & Gamble. The rear-enders, the great wealth destroyers, were usually the highly capital intensive steel and auto companies. At one point in the 1990s, IBM, once a star performer, fell to the 1,000th place, just before Lou Gerstner became CEO.

The annual article in *Fortune* analyzed the changes in the list and once again explained the value of the MVA and EVA concepts. The article also included our data on the first 200 companies on the list, as well as a shorter list of the lowest ranking companies. The full list was printed and analyzed in the pages of the *EVAngelist*, with the article also providing short accounts of companies with successful EVA programs. Reprints of these articles were widely distributed, as was other promotional material. Before long, we were also spending $1,000,000 a year advertising in the business press.

Free publicity was better. It did not have the self-serving quality of advertising; the fact that one was given a platform by a disinterested party enhanced one's credibility—and, of course, it came at no cost. I accepted as many speaking engagements as I could fit into my schedule and was usually available for interviews. I urged my colleagues to be equally available. Staff members with particular expertise in banking, the extractive industries, or retail trade, for example, were urged to contribute to trade journals and to appear on industry forums. Our Senior Management Seminars, held in different cities around the country, introduced EVA to hundreds of top executives. For those who wanted to study the subject in depth, we distributed copies of Bennett Stewart's book at the seminars and later Al Ehrbar's book, *EVA—The Real Key to Creating Wealth*, a play on the title of the 1993 *Fortune* article.

When we expanded abroad—after our Johannesburg office in 1995, London came in 1997, and the others in quick succession—we would make our first big promotional splash in a country by compiling an MVA performance list for its leading corporations and persuade a prestigious local publication to publish it. In London, for example, the list first appeared in the *Sunday Times;* in France, in *L'Expansion.* The local offices sponsored seminars on the U.S. model, and our country chief was generally favored by welcoming interviews in the local media. There was a lot of curiosity about what the newcomer from the States was proposing.

Clients came to us in a variety of ways. Some had their curiosity piqued by reading an article or attending a seminar. Financial types are great fans of technical seminars—the thirst for knowledge is well-nigh universal, perhaps in happy combination with a desire to get out of town. When the seminar attendees returned home, they would talk up the novel approach to their colleagues, and Bennett or I would soon get a call to present our case to top management. Referrals also came from satisfied clients, who introduced us to other companies. Or an executive who had a favorable experience with EVA might migrate to another company and persuade his new colleagues to give us a shot. That's what happened with William Trubeck, who was CFO of SPX Corporation in Muskegon, Michigan, when EVA was introduced in 1995. After several months, Trubeck departed to take up the same post at International Multifoods, headquartered in Wayzata, Minnesota. The company had been squandering capital at a prodigious rate, and Trubeck readily persuaded CEO Gary Costley to adopt EVA.

Perhaps our oddest entrée to a company was at Armstrong World Industries, of Lancaster, Pennsylvania, a long-established manufacturer of floor and ceiling coverings. We were the beneficiary of a foiled hostile takeover, the only time this happened to us. The tale began in 1989, when Armstrong found itself besieged by a Canadian family named Belzberg. The Belzbergs planned to get control of Armstrong with a tender offer. But when the junk bond market collapsed, the Belzbergs could not finance the offer and instead started a proxy fight to elect three candidates to the board of directors. Armstrong had cumulative voting, a system that enables dissidents to concentrate all their votes behind a favored candidate. One of the minority representatives won—none other than Professor Michael Jensen, my old friend and classmate from graduate school days. At board meetings, it was no surprise that Jensen pressed for a value-based strategy to lift the company's share price. "Jensen's whole point was that a company had to earn more than its cost of capital, and he pounded the table and made us listen," assistant treasurer Warren Posey recalled later. A five-man committee was set up to study the matter; and some months later, with the strong support of George Lorch, the new CEO, the call went out to Stern Stewart to install an EVA program.

The best magnets to attract new clients were prestigious companies with early and long success in using EVA. Briggs & Stratton (B&S), Milwaukee's pride, was one of our most successful cheerleaders, for the old-line company, founded in 1908, was well-known for probity, product excellence and sustained profitability—until it ran into trouble in the late 1980s and turned to EVA. B&S was—and is—the world's largest manufacturer of air-cooled gasoline engines, used to power all kinds of lawn mowers. It has always been highly capital intensive; and in the 1980s it spent substantial sums on automation without realizing the promised benefits. A unionized operation, it also had high labor costs. As the decade wore on, it faced enhanced competition both from Japanese imports and from a domestic rival. By the end of the 1989 fiscal year on June 30, B&S reported a loss of more than $20 million—its first red ink since the 1920s.

Management, however, had foreseen the dismal news and in 1988 had hired Stern Stewart to analyze the wisdom of asset sales or spin-offs, as well as the practicality of a leveraged buyout by the company's top executives, for there was some fear of a hostile takeover. In the end, the company rejected all these gambits and instead asked us to implement EVA. The goal was to reduce drastically the use of capital and to lower labor costs. In tandem with EVA, the company instituted strategic changes, of which the most important was to concentrate its energies on the high-volume production of low-cost engines, which it now regarded as its core business. Structural changes accompanied this reordering of priorities, with the aim being to give subordinate units considerable autonomy in operating decisions and in applying EVA.

Thus the EVA discipline was projected deep into the organization, making managers down the line aware of the need to conserve capital. Blue-collar workers were enlisted in group efforts to produce economies in the manufacturing process. Incentive plans were put into effect that covered all levels of the organization. Results were impressive. In fiscal year 1989, before EVA went into effect, the company had a negative EVA of $62 million. By FY1993, four years later, EVA moved into positive territory, with the company earning a 12.9 percent return on capital, while the cost of capital was 12 percent. In FY1999, EVA had soared to $50.9 million. Shareholders enjoyed impressive gains. Stock worth $100 in the autumn of 1990, when a share sold for $10.25, had increased to $673 in May 1999.

John Shiely, my collaborator in *The EVA Challenge*, was from the outset the prime mover in promoting EVA at Briggs & Stratton; he also had a major hand in the company's strategic reorientation. When I first met him in the early 1990s, he was president and in 2001 became CEO. His enthusiasm for EVA led him to invite visits from companies eager to see how EVA worked. Over the years, scores of companies made the trip to Wauwatosa, the Milwaukee suburb where B&S was headquartered, to be briefed by John and to tour the operation. For us missionaries, endorsements like this were invaluable.

A financial advisory firm inevitably basks in the reflected glory of its clients. Not only is the reflection heartwarming, but it also brings in new clients. Probably no EVA firm's success shone more brightly than that of SPX, which came to EVA in 1995, several years after Briggs & Stratton. At the time, SPX, then based in Muskegon, Michigan, and now in Charlotte, North Carolina, was a manufacturer of auto parts and various kinds of specialized equipment used to service motor vehicles. Historically, SPX had been a profitable company, but its earnings and stock price were still in the doldrums long after the 1991–1992 recession was over. In the summer of 1995, after I made a lengthy presentation, SPX's board decided to implement our EVA program. Equally—perhaps more—important, in December of that year, the company installed John B. Blystone as CEO. Blystone, a quick-study, high-energy dynamo of a man, had progressed up the ranks at General Electric and at the time he was hired by SPX was running two GE units in Italy.

Blystone knew little about EVA when he arrived at SPX, but he was a passionate advocate of stretch goals. "Stretch" involves the striving for goals that initially (and often in the end) appear to be unattainable but that nonetheless lead to achieving far more than could be attained by aiming for seemingly more realistic targets. In *EVA— The Real Key to Creating Wealth*, Al Ehrbar quoted Blystone as saying:

> "The whole idea of stretch is that you want people, as individuals and as a group, to do more than they, or you, can possibly understand how to achieve. Stretch goals are often considered impossible at the outset; but once you achieve the first one, it becomes the standard, and then you go on to the next level. . . . We're not going to shoot a manager for doing all the right things and still not getting a stretch goal. What we're going to shoot you for is if you set too low a target and

easily blow by it, or if you set a real tough target and then give up on it."

When Blystone arrived at SPX, the Stern Stewart team had completed the implementation of EVA. Blystone left the program intact—he particularly liked the incentive bonus plan—and over his first few months, as he toured the company, he infused it with the dynamic of stretch goals. In his first year, he cascaded the EVA incentive plan down through the organization to the shop floor. He also finished a structural reorganization of the company that had been begun by the prior management. At the same time, he pushed to rationalize operations, to improve efficiency, and, above all, to economize on the use of capital. During the course of 1996, SPX showed a $26.6 million improvement in EVA. EVA was still negative, but by far less than the minus $51 million figure of the prior year. The market was obviously aware of what was happening, for SPX's share price soared from $15.375 in January 1996 to $70.8125 eighteen months later.

In the years that followed, SPX remained a hot stock, fueled by continued EVA improvement and Blystone's irrepressible urge to expand. In the early summer of 1998, he told one visitor that he was looking for any industrial company that was underperforming and that he felt could be turned around. He had no patience with the idea that automotive parts and equipment constituted his "core competency"; he believed that his team was competent to run any industrial outfit, though not a retail or a financial firm. Remember, he came from GE.

Later in 1998, Blystone achieved his objective by buying the General Signal Corporation with a combination of cash and shares totaling $2 billion. General Signal easily qualified as an underperforming firm; in total returns, it lagged its "peer group," as well as the Standard & Poor's 500. It also was a conglomerate, with no fewer than 15 different businesses—power systems, pumps, electrical controls, and radio frequency transmission systems, among others. Absorbing General Signal bumped SPX's sales to $2.5 billion, less than half of which came from SPX.

But it was a lot to digest, and Blystone immediately announced that "SPX's leadership team intends to apply our proven EVA-based management techniques to create value in General Signal's businesses, as we've done at SPX." It was a nice tribute to EVA and we appreciated the plug—just the sort of thing to impress new prospects. Before long, we were retained again to put the General Signal business units on EVA, which meant devising new metrics and training a host of people. Three years later, SPX acquired United Dominion Industries, another medium-sized conglomerate, and again hired Stern Stewart for the same role.

From the outset, my partners and I had been impressed with SPX's prospects, particularly after John Blystone came aboard; and we took part of our fees in options on SPX stock (as we occasionally do with select companies). We had great confidence in what EVA could do for a company whose leader could rally the troops with such élan and who was so focused on expansion and real economic growth. With regard to General Signal, we took 40 percent of our fee in options exercisable 25 percent above SPX's share price. For United Dominion, we took the entire fee in options 100 percent out of the money, which meant at double the existing share price. I enjoy making our firm's statement about the quality of management. So far, I think these have been judicious decisions, despite the volatility of the stock. SPX's share price—$15.375 in January 1996, as previously mentioned—was $130 on May 3, 2002. It had been as high as $151.45 and as low as $75 in the prior 52-week period. Such volatility, of course, means high risk, and the risk finally became palpable as 2002 wore on. After a two-for-one stock split, the share price kept slipping; and by the end of February 2003, it was only in the high 30s.

The explanation was simple: SPX is principally a manufacturing company; and the recession in the manufacturing sector, which persisted after the economy as a whole started to grow in December 2001, finally caught up with it. While John Blystone's great strength has been in holding down costs and inspiring the troops, not even he could generate enough new revenue. Almost no firm is immune to a protracted recession in its field. Nonetheless, I have not wavered in my admiration for the company and for Blystone. SPX remains one of our poster companies, whose long-term success I invoke at virtually every presentation that I make to a new prospect.

Before one delivers the sales pitch, it is of course necessary to get through the door. Unless a query has come from the company, the best entrée is a referral from a mutual friend or from a satisfied client. When that is not possible, we are not at all loath to pay a finder's fee. It ranges from 2 percent of our total contract price if the finder has done no more than make the initial introduction to about 5 percent if he or she was extensively involved in the negotiations and implementation.

As our company grew, there were reversals and disappointments along the way. Winning that contract at Fletcher Challenge was a triumph at the time, as I indicated at the beginning of this chapter. We received a fee in the $1.5 million range—our highest up to that point—but in the end, Fletcher Challenge was no EVA success story. The problem was that while Sir Ronald Trotter, the chairman, was all for EVA, Hugh Fletcher, the CEO, was not. Fletcher had favored the Boston Consulting Group's CFROI program (the letters stand for "cash flow return on investment") and would have put it into effect had Sir Ronald not executed an end run by importing me from New York at the last moment.

The result was that while EVA was formally implemented, it ran into a lot of snags and resentments from managers down the line that could only have been overcome by a strenuous push from the top. At the time, I did not know that Sir Ronald and Hugh Fletcher were at loggerheads over many issues. The long-running dispute, plus strategic errors and a lot of vicissitudes, ultimately led to the break up of the company in 2001. A book entitled *Battle of the Titans—Sir Ronald Trotter, Hugh Fletcher and the Rise and Fall of Fletcher Challenge*, by Bruce Wallace, a New Zealand journalist, chronicles the sad story in great detail. I make a brief appearance in the book, characterized as a South African, which I found more than a little amusing. The error probably occurred because of my habit at the time of peppering my presentations with many examples of the success of South African EVA companies. I may also have picked up some South African locutions, but it was definitely not a case of accent.

I learned a valuable lesson from all this: an EVA program cannot succeed without the enthusiastic, unwavering support of the chief executive. The CEO must be the champion. You also need the CFO, the human resources people, and the operating heads; but the CEO can whip the entire executive suite into line. Lacking this support, it is unwise to accept the assignment, however much backing you have from the board of directors and however attractive the fee. A mediocre job will not enhance your firm's reputation.

Despite the frustration, I did have reason to be grateful to Ronald Trotter. He was also on the board of directors of the Melbourne-based ANZ Bank, as the Australia New Zealand Bank, the fourth largest in Australia, was popularly known. Sir Ronald invited me to a meeting of the bank's board to introduce the directors to EVA. The board was filled with about 20 CEOs of major Australian and New Zealand companies, so this was a tremendous opportunity for us to further our penetration into the Australian-New Zealand market. It was a major breakthrough. Sir Ronald also introduced us to Telecom New Zealand, which became a client. Telecom's chief, Dr. Roderick Deane, a former economics professor, became an ardent champion of EVA and presided over an excellent implementation. Success at Telecom led to other assignments.

More recently, we had another major disappointment, but one that in no way was of our making. It involved Visteon, the giant auto parts unit (about $19 billion in sales) of the Ford Motor Company. In 1999, Stern Stewart was hired to install an EVA program in the United States and abroad at a fee of $5.5 million a year for three years—$16.5 million in all, a large assignment for us. Visteon's management was enthusiastic about our program, which I had outlined at a company conference in Europe; and as our team set to work, I was hopeful that if we did a good job we could ultimately win a contract with the Ford Motor Company itself.

It was not to be. In April 2000, Ford announced that it would spin off Visteon to Ford shareholders, just as GM had done the year before with its Delphi auto parts company. Even before the announcement, we had been aware of what was happening and were worried when three of our strong supporters at Visteon—the CFO, the head of human resources, and the strategy chief—were reassigned to other jobs at Ford. But Visteon's president, Craig Mulhauser, kept reassuring us that Visteon would continue with EVA. When the official announcement of the spin-off came that day in April, Mulhauser resigned. Peter Pestillo, a vice chairman of Ford, well-known for his astute handling of labor relations, was installed as Visteon's new chief executive.

We still had our contract, of course, and our team in the field, headed by senior vice president David Berkowitz. The obvious thing for us to do was to get acquainted with our new clients and explain the program we were installing. I tried to make an appointment with the new CFO, but got nowhere. Then I vainly sought a meeting with Pestillo. The telephone exchange ended with that hoary message of his assistant to mine: "Don't call us. We'll call you." Clearly, the new management had no interest in EVA.

Meantime, Berkowitz, busy with his training program, was stirring up enthusiasm for EVA among the operating managers, hoping that their support would impress those at the top. It did not happen. We were also aware of another disquieting development. After the spin-off, Visteon's blue-collar workers would effectively remain employees of the Ford Motor Company, enjoying the same high wages and generous benefits of other Ford union members. The arrangement was similar to a company leasing workers from a temporary-help agency, except that it was not temporary and a union was involved. That would not in itself have vitiated an EVA program, but it would certainly have complicated it.

A few months after the announcement of the spin-off, Visteon asked us to reduce the size of the program, and thus the monthly fee. We could have refused, threatened a suit if they had insisted, and probably settled for $2 million or $3 million. But we still wanted to win over the new management, and so we agreed to the reduction. That is the dilemma faced by a consulting firm when a client's management changes. In this case, we clearly erred. A few months later, Visteon canceled the contract and we felt we had no recourse. It remained a lesson to ponder.

7

The Key Role
of Incentives

I am not an economic determinist. The fate of nations is not wholly
determined by their economic organization, resources, economic
aspirations, and rivalries. Other factors play key roles, not the
least of which are the long arm of history, ethnic conflicts, national-
ist passions. Similarly, I do not believe that man lives by bread alone.
In their daily activities, people are visibly motivated by love, patriot-
ism, religious fervor, artistic aspirations, and even a craftsman's pride
in a job well done. Nonetheless, in running a business, in motivating
people to perform well at work, nothing is more important than
monetary incentives. What kind of incentives? A rising salary scale
paralleling the promotional ladder provides a basic incentive in any
business. But it is not enough. Far more important is variable pay—
pay dependent on performance—at every step of the ladder. And
not just a modest amount—not just the 15 percent or so that I used
to inveigh against in my years at Chase. In my last two years there,
1981 and 1982, when my salary was $90,000, I bargained hard and
got a 100 percent bonus (based on the performance of my division),
but I could not get close to that for my talented staff.

We changed all that at Stern Stewart, where variable pay is a significant amount of even the most junior employee's total compensation and where for the higher ranks it is designed to exceed base salary by at least 75 percent for target performance. This generosity—a self-interested generosity, to be sure—has fueled our success. But before describing our internal system, let me outline the bonus plan we offer our clients, for our own arrangements have a couple of necessary modifications from the template.

The plan we recommend differs markedly from the common practice in most American corporations. To start with, our plan is, of course, based on EVA, the best available measure of economic performance, as I suggested in Chapter 6, rather than on such traditional measures as earnings per share. In Chapter 3, I described how EPS can be readily manipulated, which makes it a poor performance measure on which to base variable pay. Even worse is operating earnings, which some companies use, for it is frequently possible to boost this number by squandering capital on excessive expansion, whose returns might be immediate but clearly insufficient to earn the cost of capital.

Some bonus systems are based on return on net assets (RONA). This makes more sense, because capital is central to the equation. But there is still a drawback—RONA could be increased just by the sale of assets, so long as profitability is not proportionately reduced; or a potentially profitable expansion could be rejected to avoid a temporary dip in RONA. The obvious shortcomings of RONA are apparent both when RONA is below the cost of capital and, more surprising, when it is above the cost of capital. If RONA is, say, 8 percent and the cost of capital is 12 percent, then all projects above 8 percent improve RONA even if they earn less than 12 percent. If, however, RONA is, say, 19 percent and the goal is to maintain or improve RONA, then all projects above 12 percent but less than 19 percent will be rejected even though they create value.

A bonus based on EVA improvement has none of these drawbacks, for the EVA number reflects the true economic condition of the firm. In our model plan, targets are established for EVA improvement for three or five years into the future. This is in sharp variance from the practice in most non-EVA companies, where bonuses are the result of a negotiating process between superior and subordinate. In these encounters, there is a good deal of pulling and hauling that results in a compromise figure that is often below what might be achieved with greater effort. Moreover, inasmuch as the bonus is usually "capped" to a specific percentage of base pay, there is no incentive to exceed the target, which could also be taken as an indication that it was set too low in the first place.

In the EVA system, there is no room for annual bargaining because of the three- or five-year schedule of targets. The achievement of the annual EVA improvement target brings the full target bonus, which typically translates to 100 percent of salary for top executives down to 10 percent for the lowest ranking employees. If the annual EVA target is not reached—if, say, only 60 percent or 70 percent is achieved—the bonus is reduced proportionately. Below a certain achievement figure, depending on the plan, there is no bonus. On the other hand, the plan is "uncapped." If EVA performance exceeds the target, an "excess" bonus is paid. It can be twice or three times the regular bonus; the sky's the limit, literally. This is an essential ingredient of the plan, designed to elicit maximum effort.

Not all of the declared bonus is paid out for the year, however. A portion is retained in a so-called "bonus bank." Its purpose is to ensure a long-term perspective on the part of top executives and other employees, for if a good year is followed by a down year, the bonus bank is debited for the shortfall. Having money at risk is a great spur to effort; in fact, an owner's effort is more closely tied to at-risk monies than it is to the legal niceties, such as share certificate and legal title. The bonus bank also counters any impulse to boost results one year to the detriment of later years.

There are two basic types of bonus bank. In one, the target

bonus is immediately disbursed, but one-third of the "excess" bonus is deposited in the bank. Then, in each ensuing year, one-third of all funds in the bank is distributed. In the second type of bonus bank, the "all-in" bank, all bonus money is deposited in the bank, with one-third distributed each year. For the first year, the bank may be pre-funded, or the payout percentage is made larger to smooth payouts over time. I prefer the "all-in" bank, for more money is at risk, which is a more emphatic incentive, even though, if things go well year by year, the one-third annual payout increases as deposits build up in the bank.

There are other features in the all-in plan worth noting. EVA improvement does not solely mean increases in positive EVA. For companies that start the plan with negative EVA, improvement means less-negative numbers and brings the same rewards. Because the potential rewards are greatest for the largest improvement, the most capable managers are encouraged to work on the most difficult assignments requiring huge improvements. Moreover, the plan has great flexibility. While the bonuses of the top executives are based on the EVA performance of the entire firm, employees below are largely or wholly compensated on the performance of their respective units. Focusing employees on local results rewards them for what is true discretionary performance. But division managers typically have 75 percent of their bonus based on divisional EVA and 25 percent on overall corporate EVA. Why not 100 percent on the divisional numbers? The aim is to promote cooperation between division chiefs, rather than a rivalry heedless of the general welfare. Moreover, good ideas generated in one unit will more likely be quickly communicated to other units. Below the level of division heads, bonuses tend to be based 100 percent on unit performance, as far down in the organization as possible. The whole idea is to link incentives to activity that the employee can directly affect.

This is why such an incentive plan is infinitely better than profit-sharing plans, based on a firm's overall performance, and is better than the mass distribution of stock options to employees. Profits from options, after all, depend on the markets' valuation of the entire corporation's future profit picture, which the average employee is in no position to influence. Moreover, EVA bonuses are not as much affected by the fluctuations of the markets, which often reflect the general state of the economy.

The same principles underlie our incentive system at Stern Stewart. We practice what we preach, though there are some differences, due to the kind of organization we are. As a service business, we operate with a tiny amount of capital, so for all practical purposes our EVA is virtually synonymous with profitability. (Remember that EVA is derived by deducting a capital charge from NOPAT—net operating profit after tax.) More important, we are structured in such a fashion that it is easy to link incentives to an individual's direct responsibility.

We are organized by divisions, which are generally geographic but sometimes by subject, such as banking and financial services. Due to our high degree of decentralization, the variable pay for employees is based solely on divisional results. The Johannesburg office, for example, usually has nothing to do with what goes on in Singapore or in Melbourne. Occasionally, when a large assignment involves two or more offices, the bonus money is shared among those who work on the project. Such has been the case with a global grocery organization headquartered in Europe, which retained us to implement EVA in Europe, South America, and the United States.

The chief executive of each division receives a fixed percentage each year (we call it a "participation") of the EVA generated by his division, after his subordinates have gotten their share—an important point. Thus, after the staff receive 10 percent or 15 percent of the divisional EVA, the division chief is allocated between 10 percent and 25 percent of what remains. (The percentage depends on how much time Bennett Stewart or I have to spend supervising the division.) All this is not as complicated as it sounds. To illustrate: if EVA comes to

100 and the staff gets 10 percent, the division chief receives 10 percent to 25 percent of the remaining 90 percent, which comes to 9 percent to 22.5 percent of the total. What happens to the rest of the pie? It is distributed to the partners, who are ultimately responsible for running the entire firm.

For employees, the percentage of variable pay to total pay depends on rank. It can be substantial. For vice presidents, for example, the target bonus is 100 percent of base salary. Thus, a vice president earning $135,000 will receive a target bonus of $135,000. A senior vice president's target bonus is 175 percent of salary, which translates base pay of, say, $150,000 into total pay of $412,500 if the target is achieved. The bonus percentage declines as one descends the ranks, but the lowest category still get bonuses that are typically 20 percent or 30 percent of salary.

We distribute 25 percent of bonuses in December of the year earned, with the remaining 75 percent paid out in the following year. We believe in as much transparency as possible, if only to motivate people, with the result that when a large account comes in, the staff can roughly calculate the impact on their bonuses. Employees know the fee structure as well as our cost structure, and thus they can estimate the level of profitability and from that derive their approximate bonuses. Forecasts of that sort are good for morale, at least when business is good.

In two particulars, the Stern Stewart plan differs from the model we urge for our clients. For one thing, we do not set EVA improvement targets three or five years in advance. The reason is that ours is a business without a long-term client base to which we can sell additional product year by year. Typically, we get an assignment to implement EVA in a company and finish the task within eight or nine months for a medium-sized firm or within a year or two for a giant organization. In a few cases, we are brought back to do some refresher training or, as in the case of the SPX Corporation, to install

EVA in newly acquired companies. But essentially we sell one-shot operations. This makes it difficult for us to project where we should be three years hence and to set EVA improvement targets accordingly.

Partly for the same reason, we do not have a bonus bank. Building a business out of one-shot operations puts our people at a high enough level of risk as it is. Moreover, there is no need in our kind of business to enforce a long-term perspective, the primary reason for a bonus bank. With a business dependent on single assignments, we are not likely to prejudice the future in order to inflate the current year's profits. We couldn't if we wanted to.

The partners at Stern Stewart can be said to have another incentive plan of their own—stock options granted by client firms for part of our fee. Where we are optimistic about the prospects of a client, we are eager to risk present gain for future reward. The program, which began in 1995, has been astonishingly successful. We realized a profit of $16,767,000 in just five years on the options of three companies—Silicon Valley Bancshares, SmithKline Beecham, and Herman Miller, Inc.—having given up $1,650,000 in fees to secure the options.

As of May 28, 2002, we held options on the shares of 12 client companies, for which we gave up $5,359,324 in fees. We had $2,513,334 in unrealized gains, so we were behind at that date, but the option periods still had several years to run. (I should add that when we exchange part of the fee for options, our employees' bonus plans do not suffer; the full fee is used in the EVA calculations.)

The options that we hold tend to be for five years to ten years, but they cannot be exercised for the first two years, the period that we calculate will be required for the share price to reflect significantly the changes brought about by EVA. Moreover, this provision assures the client that we will not opportunistically take advantage of an unexpected upsurge in the share price to cash out; it also proves that we believe in the client's future. The two-year provision amounts to a kind of certification by Stern Stewart to the market, for we ask companies to mention the terms of the options as well as our fee in their press releases announcing that we have been retained. In the case of SPX, as I said earlier, we had two tranches of options—the first in 1998 and the second in 2001, when we were so buoyant over the long-term future of the company that we took the entire $800,000 fee in 10-year options with a strike price of $184 at a time when the market price was $92.

The option also has an escape clause—a provision that if the person who sponsored the EVA program (generally the CEO or the CFO) leaves the company, we can exchange our options for the portion of the fee that we relinquished. Under such circumstances, we would obviously have grave doubts that the program would be successful. On only one occasion have we had to invoke this provision.

I cannot exaggerate the importance of this bundle of incentives, both to ourselves and to our clients. To convince clients of the wisdom of our ideas, it was only sensible to have our own staff breathe the same air. Beyond that, we could not have attracted a talented staff without holding forth the prospect of bountiful rewards. As for our clients, a fully articulated bonus system is an essential part of an EVA implementation. To use EVA only as a measurement tool is little more than an intellectual exercise. It will not change executive behavior in a way that enhances value. There must be a link between performance and personal reward.

8

The Missionary Way of Life

I've been called a missionary, and I don't balk at the term. In 2001, for example, I carried my message to five continents and 17 countries. I can hardly lay claim to the deprivations suffered by less fortunate missionaries. I was never felled by tropical disease or kidnapped by guerrilla fighters (although I was once robbed at gunpoint, as previously mentioned). I flew first class, stayed at good hotels and ate superbly. But the pace has been rugged and often numbingly exhausting.

During the course of 2001, I made four trips to Australia, two to India, five to South Africa, nine to Turkey, ten to the United Kingdom, four to Italy, three to the Netherlands, two to Germany, two to France, three to Sweden, three to Switzerland, one to Slovakia, one to Austria, one to Belgium, one to Portugal, and one to Israel. In the United States, I flew eight times to Pittsburgh, three times to Chicago, three times to Los Angeles, twice to Cleveland, twice to Milwaukee, once to Detroit, once to San Francisco, once to Charlotte, North Carolina, and once to Greensboro, North Carolina.

Some psychiatrists maintain that this frantic scurrying about can be a symptom of profound neurosis. Individuals afflicted with this ailment habitually suppress their inner demons by getting on planes and flying to distant parts, sometimes repeating the process immediately upon arrival. That's hardly my problem. I have my own quirks, but travel is not my therapy. I am what might be called a "serious" jet-setter (as distinguished from the frivolous types who populate tabloid gossip columns). I dash about to sell ideas, and most specifically the services of Stern Stewart & Co., as well as to learn about competing ideas. This means not only making presentations to prospective clients, but also keeping up with old contacts, counseling new clients who are starting EVA programs, lecturing at business schools, attending scholarly forums and all manner of professional conferences—in other words, making myself visible in venues where business opportunities often pop up. As for new ideas, some of the most original, clever, and useful ones come from faculty colleagues at graduate business schools.

Since 2000, I have been the partner responsible for Europe; and I have long had similar responsibility for our work in South Africa, India, and Australia, although we have talented staff in each of these places. A heavy travel burden is thus inevitable—18-hour overnight trips from New York to Cape Town via Johannesburg or 12-hour overnight from London to Joburg, or well over 24 hours in transit if you fly directly from New York to Sydney. On the return trip, of course, you pick up a day when you cross the international date line, arriving in New York the same day that you leave Sydney, but the body's clock is not fooled.

On a typical trip in 2002, on May 26 I flew overnight from New York to Istanbul, changing planes in London; spent two days in Istanbul; flew to Munich on May 29; at 6:45 A.M. the following morning left for Amsterdam; took a taxi to Rotterdam; attended (and spoke at) a seminar at Erasmus University; addressed a group of graduate students the following morning; and at 9 P.M. departed for Cape Town via Johannesburg, arriving at 10:50 A.M. on June 1. The good news is that a weekend of recovery followed. There was a business meeting on Monday, then a late afternoon flight to Joburg, several meetings there and a seminar given by the Institute of Chartered Accountants, after which I flew back to Cape Town, arriving at 11:15 P.M. and renting a car to take me to my hotel. More meetings and three more nights in Cape Town, or rather in the suburb of Camps Bay, where I stayed at the Bay Hotel, my favorite hostelry in the area. On Saturday, June 8, I had to fly to Johannesburg to catch a plane to Sydney.

Monday was free; on Tuesday I was back and forth by air to Melbourne, where we have an office; then I spent two and one-half more days at meetings in Sydney; and on Friday morning, June 14, I flew to Singapore. My sole mission in Singapore was to have lunch the following day with Alan Thompson, who heads our Singapore office. Alan had recently been elected partner, and I wanted to congratulate him in person. That night I flew to London; went on to Zurich on Monday, June 17; thence to Paris for two days, Amsterdam for a night and a day, and then a flight back to New York on Friday, June 21. In 27 days, I had been to eight countries and 12 cities, some more than once, on four continents.

I'm often asked how I keep up the pace. Well, I enjoy the work. And there are quiet interludes. I've already spoken of the charms of Cape Town and its environs. Istanbul is a culturally rich city that, with its hills and minarets, resembles San Francisco as you approach it from the water. It is an exciting place to explore and I love to shop the bazaars for ceramics; I now have a handsome collection of traditional Turkish vases, candlesticks, and serving platters, mostly in blue and white. There are relaxed pleasures when the day's or week's work is done in Paris or London—a summer evening's stroll in Mayfair, for example, followed by a quiet dinner. And who can complain of a brief sojourn at the George V in Paris or the Baur Au Lac in Zurich?

Getting there is a chore and a bore, of course. The New York-London leg was easy when the schedule allowed you to take the

Concorde; with a 3½-hour flight, you could leave London in the morning and make lunch in New York; or you could leave New York after breakfast and make dinner in London, even with the time difference against you. I resumed flying the plane without hesitation after it returned to service following the fatal crash in Paris. But now all of this will only be a memory, with Concorde shut down by the time this appears in print. The real problem, of course, involves those long overnight flights; but I've worked out a way to make them tolerable, if not pleasant. The night before the flight, I purposely get little sleep, then work all day. I'm exhausted by the time I get to my seat. I tell the stewardess to delay my dinner until I ask for it, and I then fall asleep, sometimes before takeoff. I wake up two hours or so later, eat dinner, and then doze off again. I can't sleep continuously, but catnaps get me through the long night. I just do not do the reading that I planned.

I've also worked out a system to get on and off the plane quickly. I try not to check anything, for fear that a bag might be lost at the start of a long trip. This actually happened to me only once, in the late 1970s, when I was working for Chase Manhattan. Randy Earman, who was in charge of the Philippines for Chase, invited me to Manila to address some business groups on my standard subject matter. At the time, Pan American had two round-the-world flights a day from New York, leaving around the same time, one going east and one going west. I took the latter flight, but my suitcase was put on the eastbound flight. When I arrived in Manila, I was told that my bag had ended up in Paris and that it would take three days to reach me.

I had suits in my carry-on garment bag; but I needed shirts, undergarments, and socks, which Pan Am would of course pay for. So off I went in Randy Earman's chauffeured car to an elegant haberdashery. When asked my size, I said "medium," for I then weighed 150 pounds. This being the Philippines, I should have said "extra large." When I got back to the hotel, I found that the collars fit as did the bottom shirt buttons. But I couldn't fasten the buttons in between, thereby displaying about two inches of undershirt. Fortunately, I had also bought some ties, which were at least four inches wide for most of their length and could cover the gap if I didn't move around too much. But I always gesticulate when I'm lecturing, and a single arm flung upward betrayed me. My suitcase finally showed up.

Several years ago Bennett Stewart was similarly victimized. We were scheduled for a joint appearance in Singapore. Out of the same anxiety that parents sometimes have about flying on the same plane, we decided to take separate flights. I flew west and he flew east, through Europe. We arrived at approximately the same time, but Bennett was bereft of his bags. They turned up a few days later.

I do not use porters, but I must look like one myself, scurrying to the gate with a suitcase on wheels, a briefcase mounted on the suitcase, and a garment bag draped over both. If the ticket agent insists on checking the suitcase, I at least will have the garment bag in the cabin, in which I've packed two suits and a three-day supply of linen—just in case. Also, I'm wearing a blazer, slacks, shirt, and tie. The slacks are of a kind that don't wrinkle much, so I am ready for all contingencies upon alighting from the plane. Some of my fellow travelers in first class seem to be dressed in work clothes or beach attire, which mildly offends my sense of decorum. Forgive me if this sounds old-fashioned, but I do believe that most people look better fully dressed than half dressed.

I also like hats, in all seasons. They keep the head warm or shielded from the sun; and, if properly selected in regard to facial contour and head size, they look good. I'm old enough to remember when a man or woman was not fully dressed without a hat. The late Alex Rose, the president of the hatter's union, would have loved me. He was always trying to get public figures to wear hats—to be cranial role models. (Rose, who ran New York's Liberal Party, would not have approved of my politics, however, nor I of his.) In one particular, I am a rebel boy. I hate to wear a dinner jacket and do not routinely pack one. I think that men in black tie—let alone white tie—act unnaturally. Perhaps it is the uniform that offends my sense of individuality.

The briefcase that I carry on my travels is of my own design and resulted from a chance meeting on a plane with a South African who manufactured leather goods. We were seated together and fell to chatting about his business, whereupon I began to complain about briefcases. The standard designs, I maintained, had an insufficient number of pockets and pockets that were too small for their contents. Attaché cases also left much to be desired. Intrigued, my companion asked me to describe my ideal briefcase. I took out a pad and sketched a case nine and one-quarter inches long and wide, with pockets large and small, inside and out, to accommodate papers, a book or two, and passport and tickets in appropriate compartments. He said he would have it made for me. The ideal case arrived decked out in black ostrich leather, with both shoulder strap and handle, and was well worth the price of $800. I have used this bag for more than eight years with no visible signs of wear and tear.

At the time of writing, I have been flying for 37 years, and I've never ceased to marvel at the miracle of it. Even a knowledge of aerodynamics, of which I have a smattering, does not diminish one's awe at the annihilation of distance. During those 37 years, there have been a few mishaps, but not enough to threaten the serenity I feel at six or seven miles above the earth. There was the time several years ago when I was flying to Dayton, Ohio, from New York. The plane was descending normally for landing when it suddenly shot upward as if it had been catapulted. The pilot came on to say, surprisingly mildly, "My gosh, we'll have to report that air traffic controller." He explained that the runway was a mile away. Then the plane made a full circle and came down gently onto the concrete. I understand that on press planes the journalists often applaud after a landing, but we were too stunned.

I had a more frightening experience in the mid-1980s on a flight from Los Angeles to New York. As we were leaving Los Angeles, instead of flying out over the water and then heading east, the plane circled the airport and came down low over the control tower. The pilot came on the loudspeaker and explained that the plane's landing gear had not retracted, and he also could not lower it. For some reason, it was locked, and he wanted a visual inspection from the control tower with binoculars. The tower told him that the landing gear was extended three-quarters of the way. The pilot explained that if he could not get the landing gear down by the time we reached New York, he would have to crash-land the plane. The atmosphere in the cabin was tense, as you might imagine. Nobody had any interest in eating or watching the movie. One woman near where I sat panicked and I helped quiet her. The pilot walked around the aisles, trying to reassure us and responding to a hare-brained plan that some passengers favored—to avoid a crash landing by ditching the plane in the ocean. The pilot explained that at all costs we wanted to avoid the water. The plane would sink like a rock.

When we arrived in New York, he again flew low over the control tower. The landing gear was still locked in the three-quarter position. The pilot told us that the airport would lay a blanket of foam on the runway to try to prevent a fire and that he would land with the nose of the plane tilted upward, so that the wheels could hit the ground. Nonetheless, he said, the wheel carriage would collapse, and the plane would be sliding in on its belly. He then dumped the excess fuel in the ocean before attempting to land. As the plane descended, we could see fire engines and emergency vehicles lined up all along the runway. It was scary, to say the least. We landed and we were lucky—there was no fire. But we still slid down chutes to reach the ground.

In May 2002, I had another bizarre experience. I was flying a British Airways Boeing 777 from London to New York. After I was seated, I filled out a customs declaration and placed it with my passport on a shelf near my seat. When the plane took off, I was suddenly aware that the documents were sliding along the shelf in the reverse direction to the thrust of the plane. Before I could retrieve them, passport and customs declaration disappeared down a crevice at the rear of the shelf. I told a stewardess of my plight, she informed the cockpit, and after we landed in New York, a couple of mechanics came aboard. They dismantled some sections of the wall and found the customs declaration, but no passport. It was heavier than the customs paper and had disappeared into the bowels of the plane. What to do? I was finally told I had to get off the plane, and I suddenly felt like one of those stateless people who shuttle between airports unable to be admitted anywhere. On the ground, however, a sympathetic British Airways agent told me that she had talked to customs and that all they needed was my name, date of birth, and address, and they could look me up in the computer. By the time I got to passport control, they had my passport number and I was admitted. A day or two later, I had to go to the Post Office and apply for a duplicate passport and then get new visas for Turkey and India.

Among the pleasures of air travel are the people you meet on planes, although one has to be cautious in responding to conversational overtures. I think I've developed a sixth sense as to who's likely to be garrulous or confessional or both and am likely to be clipped in my responses and quickly bury myself in my papers. The ultimate defense, of course, is to fall asleep, but one cannot readily do that while eating. I've never gone so far as an English gentleman who sat down next to a friend of mine in first class and announced that he was not talkative. My friend replied that he would not dream of intruding on the man's privacy. They sat in silence for hours as the plane droned across the Atlantic, but finally the Englishman spoke up. He asked to borrow my friend's copy of the *Economist*. My friend handed it to him without saying a word. He had won the contest.

Sometimes an airborne conversation leads to business, which is why I don't suppress my normal gregariousness. Unless I'm sitting next to that little old lady from Dubuque, I make an effort to learn what field my neighbor is in. I'm graceful about inquiring, leading up to the question through some transitional exchanges. I hate the abrupt "What do you do?" that one is assailed with at cocktail parties. (I have a friend who responds, "As little as possible.") The Concorde was perhaps the best venue for these discreet inquiries, for it was usually filled with CEOs and CFOs. For some reason, I don't pursue much conversation with rock stars or sports personalities, although I did once ask Bjorn Borg for some tips about selecting a tennis racquet. After my neighbor responds to my query, he or she invariably asks the same question of me, and I soon launch into an exposition of EVA and its varied advantages for all manner of companies. On a Concorde trip from New York to London in 1996, I found myself seated next to a man named Tom Vidar Rygh, who turned out to be a senior executive of Orkla, a diversified Norwegian consumer goods company with a large investment portfolio. He told me about his business, I told him about mine, and he expressed an interest in looking further into EVA. Some time elapsed before we arranged a formal meeting, which ultimately led to a presentation to the company's top management and a substantial contract to install an EVA program.

On another occasion in the spring of 2000, I was on one of two queues waiting to board the Concorde in London when I suddenly found myself face-to-face with Sir Martin Sorrell, who was on the other queue. Cordial greetings all around; we had met several years before, when I had vainly tried to get him to adopt EVA. He heads the WPP Group, a holding company that owns several large advertising and PR companies. WPP had recently acquired Young & Rubicam, an old-line New York ad agency. For months, Stern Stewart had been negotiating with Y&R to set up a joint venture to market a new product called BrandEconomics, of which more later. The talks had initially gone well, but they were now in abeyance. Our people could no longer even get their phone calls returned. I suspected that the Y&R types were so preoccupied with the merger, which would allow them to cash in their options at a considerable profit, that they had little interest in much else.

After we boarded the plane, I acted on this opportunity. I walked over to Sorrell's seat and handed him a note, in which I described the problem and said that if we could not make a deal with Y&R, we would approach another advertising agency with a similar data base and try to set up a joint venture with them. A few minutes later Sorrell was at my seat. He promised that before the day was out (the Concorde was due to land at 9:30 A.M.), he would have his people call my people. He did so. The negotiations, in which both of us got personally involved, were protracted. In the end, we did not set up a joint venture but worked out a licensing agreement that enabled us to launch the new business in February 2002.

My most memorable chance encounter on a plane occurred early in 1982, when I was still working for the Chase Manhattan Bank. I was on a flight from New York to Phoenix, with a stop in Dallas. I was in coach, having been unable to get a first-class ticket, and was sitting in an aisle seat. When the Dallas passengers started to board, I was absorbed in a book; and when a woman approached my row, I did not glance up but simply slung my legs over the arm rest so that she could pass. Some time after the plane was aloft again, she left her seat, and I repeated my leg maneuver and again did not look at her. But when she returned, I glanced up, caught my breath, and exclaimed with the impetuosity of a schoolboy, "I must be stupid!"

She laughed. "Either that or it's a very good book."

That remark impressed me. She was obviously bright and quick, and not only gorgeous but a true Latin beauty—dark eyes, olive complexion, and lustrous black hair—with a smile that left an onlooker weak in the knees. Dolores (not her real name) and I talked animatedly all the way to Phoenix. She was a college student from Texas who had won a beauty contest sponsored by a trade association and was traveling around the country promoting its products before business groups. I told her what I did, and she asked intelligent questions. As the plane taxied to the gate, I said, "You know, unless we make some plans, we're not likely to see each other again."

"I guess not," she said. I was completely deflated.

But we caught up with each other at the carousel, awaiting our bags. Fortunately, for this flight I had checked my luggage. I tried again, proposing that we meet in Phoenix. "But I'm completely booked," she said. "So am I," said I; but I pointed out that I had an hour after lunch before my next meeting. Perhaps we could meet then. "What would we do?" she asked. I said I knew a drugstore in town that made malts, milk shakes, and ice cream sodas just like in the movies.

She agreed.

For the rest of our time in Phoenix, we each had business dinners every night, but we avoided eating and would meet around 10 P.M. for a quiet meal together. But the idyll had to end. I had to return to New York, and she was scheduled to travel abroad for her trade group. She would not be back for six months, when she would fly into San Francisco after touring the Far East. She told me the date and I said I would meet her at the St. Francis Hotel for dinner. "But suppose you're not there," she said. "Suppose you meet someone else in the meantime."

"Then I won't be there," I said. "But I assure you I will."

Six months later, we met at the appointed time and lingered over a long meal. It was during that meal, I believe, that we fell in love. We made plans to see each other as often as possible. She had to return to Texas to start her senior year in college in September. During that year, I made several trips to Texas, and she would fly up to New York. There were 20 years between us—she was 21—but age did not matter. I was in the midst of getting Stern Stewart off the ground, a process that fascinated her. She was interested in business; indeed she was interested in almost everything. She had immense intellectual curiosity and read widely. I had the kind of companionship that I had never enjoyed in my marriage.

109

After graduation, Dolores came to New York, found a job, and also found an apartment, which was not as difficult or as expensive as it is now. We saw each other for six years, though the last two were rocky, with several breakups. There were irritants. I knew mine; doubtless she had hers. A major problem was that Erik did not like her. He complained that when we spent weekends together in East Hampton, and when I was not present, she would boss him around. I began to wonder whether she had a hidden personality that would become only too visible if we were married. Erik predicted that if we had children, she would send them to a military academy, certainly a dismal fate. Another bad omen was that my sister Roberta did not warm to her; she found Dolores cold, distant.

Religion was not the problem. From the outset, Dolores knew that I would not marry out of my faith. She was nominally a Roman Catholic, very nominally. I never urged her to convert to Judaism; but during our final period together, she began to study and finally underwent an Orthodox conversion. Soon after we broke up, she met someone else, who was also Jewish, married him, and had children. After several years, they were divorced. I still occasionally have a meal with her when I visit her town. She is still beautiful, bright, engaging; but I see her as if from a distance and have difficulty believing that I was so passionately engrossed for so long. All this from a chance meeting on a plane.

The reader might have gathered that my religion is important to me. As mentioned earlier, I come from an orthodox, meticulously observant home and attended a yesihva, hardly an unusual experience in New York City. As with many people, my religious faith was instilled in my early years. It was just a fact of daily life, accepted unquestioningly. Many people rebel in later life against early religious indoctrination. It never occurred to me to do so. While I dissented from my parents' liberal political views, as regards religion I was always a believer. Religious belief is necessarily a matter of faith. It is not subject to empirical validation or irrefutable logical proof.

My parents in their thirties.

Myself at age nine. After
I was given the baseball
cap, I wouldn't remove
it, even at bedtime.

I was 36 in this Chase Manhattan Bank ad, but who would have guessed it? (Reprinted with the permission of JPMorgan Chase & Co.)

With infant Erik, looking out at the Hudson River from our Riverdale apartment.

My parents at their sixtieth anniversary party in 1997.

My favorite picture of Erik, taken by me, outside a synagogue in Stellenbosch, South Africa.

With Bennett Stewart, my longtime partner and comrade-in-arms in the theoretical wars. (*Photo by* Yvonne Gunner.)

Erik and I were pleased to pose in 2001 with my friend Nobel laureate Gary Becker, a fellow member of the Mont Pelerin Society. (*Photo by* Yvonne Gunner.)

I was always proud to lend an arm to Peter Drucker, who was flanked by his wife. (*Photo by* Yvonne Gunner.)

With classmate Michael Jensen (left) and Julian Franks of the London Business School. (*Photo by* Yvonne Gunner.)

I hope the audience got the point. (*Photo by* Yvonne Gunner.)

Judge Mervyn King, a former member of the Supreme Court of South Africa, didn't disdain a little physical labor. (*Photo by* Yvonne Gunner.)

Lauren Bacall easily persuaded me. She spoke at an EVA Institute seminar in 1997, but not on EVA. (*Photo by* Yvonne Gunner.)

With two supporters from the United Kingdom: Professors Richard Brealey (left) and Julian Franks of the London Business School. (*Photo by* Yvonne Gunner.)

With Dr. Stefan Kirsten, CFO of Thyssen-Krupp and a member of the Stern Stewart International Advisory Board. (*Photo by* Yvonne Gunner.)

Ann-Margret charmed me and enlivened an EVA Institute seminar in Palm Beach in 2000. (*Photo by* Yvonne Gunner.)

All the proofs of the existence of G-d that we learn in an elementary philosophy course are unpersuasive to the skeptic, who wonders how finite man, with all the limitations of finiteness, can delineate the infinite.

The simplest way to put it is that religious faith is a matter of temperament. Not only did I have faith, but I took pleasure in following the laws and rituals that define a Jew's daily life. After my Bar Mitzvah, I recited my morning prayers after binding phylacteries with leather thongs to my forehead and left arm. By the time I graduated from the yeshiva, I was thoroughly conversant with the liturgy; and to this day, I am proud of the fact that I can conduct a prayer service.

I always had great respect for the counsel of our rabbis. When I was a student at the University of Chicago, I wanted to get a mezzuzah—the small case enclosing a parchment with sacred words ordained in the Bible—to tack on the doorjamb of my dormitory room. I went to a nearby synagogue and found myself talking to the rabbi. He was pleased to give me a mezzuzah, and subsequently I would call on him from time to time. We became friends. When I mentioned this relationship to my rabbi back home, he said it was fine to talk but that I must not attend a religious service in that rabbi's synagogue, for his was a conservative synagogue, where men and women sat together and a choir and organ music were part of the service. The deviations from tradition in reform congregations are even more extensive, with perhaps as much as or more prayer in English than in Hebrew and with the men going hatless. Many of the orthodox, who regard these establishments as churches, not synagogues, derogate the Jewishness of their congregants, although recognizing, of course, that by Jewish law anyone born of a Jewish mother is a Jew. It is equally true that in a non-Jewish society like our own, even a Jew who converts to Christianity is still considered by non-Jews to be a Jew. What was true in Victorian England—I'm thinking of Benjamin Disraeli, the Tory prime minister, whose father converted—is as true in our own country today, though many converts are too naïve to know it.

Orthodox Jews do not constitute a monolithic community. There are two main groups: the ultraorthodox and what some call modern orthodox. Some of the ultraorthodox are recognizable (I'm talking about the men) by their long black coats, black hats, tieless white shirts, and dangling sideburns. They belong to one of several Hassidic sects, of which the Lubavitcher is one of the most prominent. They are much more of a presence in New York City in recent years than before World War II, for large numbers of survivors emigrated here after the war, established cohesive communities and prospered. They tend to have large families and so their numbers have grown. It is commonplace in midtown Manhattan to encounter exotically dressed youngsters who, when they get within earshot, are overheard talking in unadulterated New Yorkese.

But the ultraorthodox are not limited to the Hassidim. There are others who are conventionally dressed, though they always wear a skull cap, or yarmelke (as do many of the nonultras). In some cases, the yarmelke is so small that it has to be pinned to the hair. The ultras are more diligent than the rest of us in trying to adhere to as many as possible of the 613 laws—dos and don'ts—that are supposed to regulate a Jew's behavior. Their piety is also expressed in other external ways. When the Torah is read in synagogue, for example, they will stand, whereas the rest of us will sit. On the eve of the holiday of Shevuot, which commemorates G-d's giving the law to Moses on Mount Sinai, the ultraorthodox will stay up all night studying sacred texts. The rest of us will simply appear for morning services.

The scrupulousness with which the ultras take the laws of kashruth can be breathtaking. Not long ago, I invited one of my black-robed rabbi friends to lunch at a favorite kosher Italian restaurant in midtown Manhattan. When we arrived, I asked whether he had ever been there before. "Not really," he replied. What did that mean? It turned out that the day before, he had cased the joint. He had inspected the kitchen and decided that the *mashgiach*—the man who oversees the restaurant's adherence to the rules of kashruth—had been deficient in some way. "I'll eat fish," said my friend. And so did I, but principally out of respect.

I have never aspired to ultraorthodoxy. My brand of orthodoxy, however, is not without its rigors. It requires strict observance of the sabbath and of five holidays: Passover, Shavuot, Succot (the harvest festival), Rosh Hashonah, the start of the Jewish New Year, and Yom Kippur, the Day of Atonement, 10 days later. (During that 10-day period, sinners can avoid a dismal fate through true repentance, prayer, and charity.) Great emphasis is placed on charity, not only during the 10 days of repentance but throughout the year. I have little doubt that I have done my bit, in small as well as large ways. It may be eccentric, but I never turn down a request for help. I remember once when a woman with whom I was walking remonstrated with me after I dropped a bill into an outstretched cup. "Why waste your money?" she said. "It'll only go for drink or drugs." I replied that if there was only one chance in a million that the money would be put to good use, it was worthwhile. "To us it is trivial," I said, "but to the one in need it could be everything."

I observe the holidays strictly, though I've otherwise had to make my accommodations with orthodox observance. For Passover, it has been a tradition in our family to go off for the eight-day period to a hotel that features a kosher kitchen and facilities for private and public seders. The whole family would go—my parents, my sisters with their husbands and children, and Erik, who would fly in from London. The sojourn had the quality of a relaxed retreat, but it also had the practical advantage that each housewife could avoid the chore of completely changing all the dishes and cooking utensils for the brief period and making the home strictly kosher for Passover, which means free of leavened foods. Last year's Passover had an overlay of sadness, for it was the first one without my mother, who died in January 2002.

After my mother's death, I was resolved to say kaddish—the mourner's prayer—three times every day for the period of 11 months, as ordained by law. There was no problem during the initial seven-day period of mourning, for I was in New York, with ready access to synagogues; but I have to travel. What to do? One of my rabbi friends told me that if I made a donation to a yeshiva, a student or an employee would say kaddish every day for me. As often as possible, I would, of course, say kaddish myself.

It is relatively easy to do in the United States, where I have a list of synagogues in major cities; but it is a problem if I'm flying at the time of late-afternoon and early-evening services. One can say kaddish without going to a synagogue, but you need a minyan (a quorum of 10 men), which is not easy to come by on a plane. (The bearded Hassidim in black manage it at times, for they recognize each other's uniform.) When I was in Mumbai (formerly Bombay), I thought I was in luck, for the synagogue was only a few blocks from my hotel; but I discovered that it only held services on the sabbath. Not enough men came to daily prayers. London, of course, has not been a problem. I go to the Marble Arch Synagogue in Great Cumberland Place; but when I first appeared at 7:30 A.M. for morning services, I found it was not easy to get in. A man whom I assumed was a sexton questioned me through an aperture in the door. I explained my mission. "What is your Hebrew name?" he asked. I told him. "What is your mother's Hebrew name?" I told him. "Come on in," he said, unlocking the door. The interrogation was a new security measure.

As an observant Jew, I've had to make some accommodations because of my business pursuits. I deviate somewhat from the law in my personal behavior after weighing the pluses and minuses. I may flatter myself but I think it's important to offer my services in South Africa and two days later agree to be in India, which may interfere with lesser holidays. According to the law, I should eat only in kosher restaurants, where all the dietary laws are followed. But I think it's important to take business contacts to Le Gavroche or the Connaught in London or to La Grenouille or La Cote Basque in New York. Or when I'm on the road, clients invite me for a meal, and I can't refuse. And then there's the problem of banquets. Like many others with my background, my solution is to forgo meat and only eat fish. It's probably better for my health anyway. But I do carry around with me a book listing kosher restaurants in the United States and in Europe and around the world. I go to them on my own or with kindred spirits. Air travel is of course no problem. You can always order a kosher meal in advance. (The best in first class, in my judgment, is on British Airways. Always look for the Hermolis brand.)

Someone of my persuasion is often confronted by questions from secular Jews as to why the ancient laws cannot be drastically modified or abandoned. Why is it forbidden, for example, to push a button and ride an elevator on the sabbath? Does it make any sense that the rabbis equated electricity with fire, thereby equating pushing a button with lighting a fire? The answer, basically, is the slippery-slope or the camel's-nose-under-the-tent arguments: once you start on this path of reform, where will it end? And who will be deemed the authority for making the changes? Religious faith cannot survive without ritual and without laws regulating human behavior. That is why I am not alone in regarding the orthodox community as the guarantor of the Jewish future in the United States. And I am also not alone in fearing that the high rate of intermarriage among conservative and reform Jews will lead to the ultimate disappearance of these denominations within a few generations. There is little intermarriage among the orthodox, but there is a cohesiveness and self-assurance that come from diligent adherence to law and tradition. And among the ultraorthodox, as previously mentioned, there is a high reproductive rate.

Personally, religious observance also serves as a psychological corrective to the frenetic activity of a global gadabout. While hardly the purpose of worship, the solace and calm that it brings are among its happy consequences. Enter a grand house of worship before the throng arrives, sit in the rear, and you cannot help but feel the great hush of peace descend. For a time, you shed your anxieties. The interlude is resuscitating.

I have another diversion, also a serious one, from the daily grind. That is teaching. Lecturing to a class on the fine points of financial theory is a liberating change of pace—concentrating on abstract ideas displaces mundane concerns. As previously described, I began teaching economics at night at the City College of New York and then went on to lecturing on finance to graduate students at New York University, again at night. Not the least of my motives at first was to make a little money. I also wanted to sharpen my communication skills. My father urged this effort on me, and I was long aware of how effective he was when he spoke before our congregation, if only to make a series of announcements. He was a master at holding an audience.

After I was established at Chase and began writing in financial journals in the early 1970s, I started giving courses on modern financial theory to MBA candidates at institutions as diverse as the University of Cape Town, Witswatersrand University in Johannesburg, Columbia University in New York, the University of California at Los Angeles, the University of Rochester, the London Business School, Carnegie Mellon in Pittsburgh, and the University of Michigan. I usually give a single course in the fall or the spring semester, which I am able to fit into my travel schedule with careful planning; but sometimes I have to stretch myself. In the autumn of 2001, I gave a course at Columbia on Monday afternoons and Friday mornings.

At the same time, I committed myself to teach at Carnegie Mellon on Thursday evenings. It was easy enough to fly to Pittsburgh on Thursday afternoons, but to make my 10 A.M. Friday session at Columbia, I had to take a 7 A.M. plane in Pittsburgh for New York. That meant getting up at 5 A.M.

If I occasionally happen to miss a class, I make it up with a doubleheader. The students have to be understanding. At the London Business School in April 2002, the nickname of "marathon Joel" was once again bestowed on me. I had started a course the prior January; but before I could finish it, I was called back to New York because of my mother's final illness. I was unable to complete the lectures before April, but on three days that month—April 14, 28, and 29—I taught for seven hours a day, with a lunch break, and covered the six classes I had missed in January. For students who couldn't attend, the classes were videotaped.

For the April 14 marathon, a Sunday, I had flown in from South Africa on the Saturday-night flight, arriving at 5:45 A.M. Sunday morning; on Monday morning, I was off to India. Why do I knock myself out? The first reason, obviously, is that I enjoy teaching. I enjoy not only the agreeable change of pace, as I said before, but also the contact with young minds. I guess I was born a teacher, which is certainly part of the missionary's role. I also identify with the students, for I readily remember when I was one myself. I empathize with their anxieties. For 25 years, I have asked students to write their phone numbers on their exam papers. Anybody who gets an A receives a congratulatory call from me, no matter where I am located when I complete grading the papers.

I remember years ago telephoning John M. Ferguson, a student at Columbia, to give him the good news. I reached his wife and asked for him by his full name, not knowing that everybody called him Mac. "Does my husband know you?" she asked. I assured her that he did, and she called out, "A Joel Stern wants you!" I heard a scream in the background, and he was soon on the phone. After thanking me profusely, he suddenly said, "Am I good enough for Stern Stewart?" We hired him, first as an intern one day a week while he was still studying for his degree, then as a full-time staff member. For some years now, Mac has been the partner in charge of our Latin American practice. There are several other staff members whom I first knew as students and then recruited to be employees. Both Mich Bergesen and Alan Thompson took my course at Wits in Johannesburg at different times. Mich went on to run Stern Stewart's Johannesburg office and then the London office, and he now shares responsibility with Al Ehrbar for our BrandEconomics practice. Alan Thompson succeeded Mich as head of the Johannesburg office before opening the Singapore office, from which he covers all of Southeast Asia.

Chaith Kondragunta, formerly director of our Indian office and now deputy chief of Western and Northern Europe, was a student of mine at Carnegie Mellon, where he was class valedictorian. Patrick Furtaw first came to my attention when he excelled in my class at Columbia. We hired him and watched him make our Tokyo office a success before he became head of our banking and financial services practice in New York at the end of 2002. Simeon Hyman is another former Columbia student of mine, who has had two tours of duty at Stern Stewart, applying EVA principles to retail businesses, his speciality. Recruiting the best and the brightest would be sufficient motive for all the time I spend teaching, if I required any justification, which I don't.

Despite the crowded schedule, I do have a refuge from work—my house in East Hampton on the South Fork of Long Island, about a hundred miles from Manhattan, depending on where you start measuring. I go there in all seasons when I get back to the United States, and I try to spend a few weeks there in the summer. East Hampton is a lovely place, lushly verdant with manicured lawns and hedges in the posh areas, woodsy elsewhere, with broad sandy beaches stretching behind the pounding surf on the ocean side and

calm waters on the bay side. In recent years East Hampton has figured in the gossip columns because of the large influx of movie stars,
particularly after the 1994 earthquake in the Los Angeles area; but
when I first visited it in 1979, it was better known as a resort of the
genteel rich, who had been there forever, as well as for its large population of artists and writers. Actually, it is as heterogeneous as the island of Manhattan itself, with many people of modest means.

My friend Eddie Maslow first introduced me to the delights of
East Hampton. He is an artist and an advertising man who has lived
in the area for more than 30 years, and he finally prevailed on me in
1979 to drive out to see for myself. I was so taken with the charm of
the place that I soon found myself in a real estate office, talking to a
woman named Mary Ryder. She put me in her car, and we went looking at properties. They were handsome, patrician but much too
large. I pointed out that I was alone, with a young son who lived with
his mother. I needed something more modest, whereupon Mary suggested that I buy some land and build my dream house. She showed
me two plots on Further Lane, one of the premier locations in the village, close to the ocean. One was a one-acre plot, the other three
acres. They were owned by an estate that was trying to raise cash
quickly to settle tax liabilities. I was interested in the larger plot and
asked the price. "$140,000," said Mary. Without giving it much
thought, I offered $80,000. Mary checked with the estate, and they
quickly accepted. This left me with the feeling, of course, that I had
offered too much. But I have had no regrets.

The next step was to get an architect. I was impressed with the
work of Norman Jaffe, which I had seen featured in an architectural
magazine, and counted myself lucky to be able to retain him. Getting a house built to one's own specification is an exciting adventure,
though it can be nerve-wracking if one is indecisive. But I knew what
I wanted, a house that was both spacious and cozy, dramatic yet em-
inently livable. The structure that Norman designed fulfilled my aspirations. Some 4,700 square feet, it has a stone facade and is built

around a large central space, 28 feet high, that combines living room and dining area, the latter on a slight rise in one corner. Against one wall is a huge stone fireplace that rises to the ceiling. The reverse side of the stone column provides a fireplace for the family room and another for my bedroom, to which I ascend by a long staircase. On the way up the stairs are two other landings, providing entrances to two guest bedrooms. There is another bedroom off the kitchen.

The entire interior is paneled in five-inch wide natural cedar, which adds considerable warmth. The floor is covered with two-foot squares of black slate, an arresting contrast. Outside the house are a pool, a tennis court, and a garage. The ocean is a mere 700 feet away, though I rarely go to the beach. I avoid sunbathing because of the health hazards, a subject in which I became interested years ago when I encountered a team of technicians taking ultraviolet readings in New Zealand.

The house in East Hampton offers a degree of relaxation that I get nowhere else in the U.S. When my car crosses the Shinnecock Canal, the final stage of the trip to the South Fork—the homeward journey heralded by the strains of Brahms or Mozart on the car hi-fi—a tremendous load lifts from my shoulders. The image is trite, but for me it has a physical reality. I straighten up in my seat, open the window. The air seems fresher, the sun brighter. After I park the car, I take a briefcase full of papers from the office into the house. I place the papers on a shelf, to be read later. When the weekend is over, they are largely unread.

I have five bicycles in the house and ride almost every morning. I spend a fair amount of time in the kitchen. My specialty is breakfast. I make a luscious French toast, using challah, the traditional Jewish white bread, drenched in egg batter and served with an overlay of thick maple syrup. I'm also proud of my huge pancakes, 14 inches in diameter, the size of my largest pan. The presence of guests stimulates these caloric excesses. No cholesterol tests are available or permitted chez moi. I feed the leftovers to the swans on the village pond, a daily ritual that I've followed for years. When there are no leftovers, they seem quite happy with nine-grain or twelve-grain stone-ground bread. Sometimes I can feel the swans sneer at lesser offerings.

East Hampton is best in the warm months, of course, but the year can provide two summers if one goes south. Remember that 1966 film called *The Endless Summer* about surfers who followed the sun from California through the southern hemisphere, seeking to ride the big waves throughout the year? In a small way, I've done the same thing by building a house in Camps Bay, a suburb of Cape Town. It's on the beachfront, with a great ocean view, 150 meters from the Bay Hotel, where I've stayed for years. I bought a five-story, 6,000-square-foot newly constructed building in February 2002 and hired a well-known architect, Stefan Antoni, to renovate it—a five-story atrium, an elevator from the garage level, central heating and central air-conditioning. After a few months of work, cracks were discovered in the foundation, and I was advised to demolish the house and start fresh. I've done so; and, oddly, it only cost an extra $7,000, for the renovations I had wanted were very extensive.

The Camps Bay house is due to be completed in October 2003. It will be spring then in South Africa but I will be there for winter as well for my teaching chores in July and August. So I can have endless winters as well as summers. The winters are milder by far in Cape Town than in New York. Cape Town's beauty is sufficient, but would you believe 80-to-83-degree highs in summer, with little if any humidity and no rain? Every day is gorgeous.

Please do not visit, for if you or others do, Camps Bay's delicate village atmosphere will be like Laguna Beach in California or the French Riviera.

9

Dispatches from the Sales Front

Years ago, after I won what was then considered a large contract for us, I was driven to the airport by an amiable man who worked for the company's CFO. At one point, visibly embarrassed, he told me that his colleagues felt that the price that we had agreed on—$750,000—was very high. He wondered whether it could be reduced by $25,000. I was a bit taken aback but quickly replied that prices were neither high nor low. What was relevant to price was whether you thought you could earn a fair return on your investment. "I want you to set the price," I told him. "If you want to lower it by $25,000, it's a done deal. But there will be consequences. I will not attend the steering committee meetings, and I will not monitor the project. So you decide what you want—buy what you feel is necessary." He was silent for a few moments and then said they would not dispute the price.

I felt confident in that exchange because I was on a high, knowing I had won the enthusiastic support of the company's CEO. I also had the arrogance, if you like, of believing I was representing a unique product. Any student in Management 101 knows that a highly differentiated product, satisfying a vital consumer need that is not being met, has the best chance in the marketplace. It is a truism that such a product is easier to sell than a commodity, where the emphasis has to be on price, quality, and customer service (as well as, I suppose, on the sales rep's personality and the provision of football tickets).

Since my early years in the business I have felt I was selling a product like no other. I had that conviction when I was championing the virtues of free cash flow, long before that concept won widespread acceptance, and I have had the same conviction about EVA. EVA has been so successful that it has of course become generic, as I've said earlier, but what now differentiates our product from its competitors, indeed what makes it unique, is the way we implement it. Claiming uniqueness may seem immodest, but I think our record supports the statement.

As I travel around the world, I am often asked how Stern Stewart became a global business in such a short time—how we attract clients, how we sell, how we negotiate prices. I've already touched on some of these matters and I have no hesitancy about going into more detail; I'm not worried about revealing trade secrets. Prospective clients first become acquainted with our story through reading an ad or an article about the Market Value Added rankings in their country; or they may have attended one of our periodic seminars, about which I have written at length in Chapter 3. Or they may have heard a talk before a professional gathering by me or one of my partners. As I've said before, I rarely turn down an invitation to speak if I can possibly make the date. You can never tell who will be there.

It was just such happenstance that led to my meeting David Sussman several years ago in Johannesburg. Sussman, then as now, is CEO of the JD Group, a prosperous retail chain of furniture stores. I had never sought him out, for at the time we had done little work in retail. The occasion of our meeting was a graduation dinner of the Henley business school, at which I delivered the main address and

Sussman received an award as entrepreneur of the year. It was an occasion notable, in the first instance, for Sussman's candor. He began his remarks by telling the audience, "Have you ever wondered how people like me get the alumni award? I'll tell you—I've obviously contributed too much money to the school." There was a titter in the audience; and I could see that my friend, Andy Andrews, the school's dean, was stunned. Andy looked like a wide receiver in a football game who, not seeing the ball tossed by the quarterback, was hit on the head and fell to the ground.

Anyway, when the speaking was over, Sussman leaned across the table and said he had been looking forward to meeting me for a long time. Pleasantly surprised, I asked why, and he said that he had read the 1993 *Fortune* article about EVA and had been much impressed by it. He then invited me for dinner at his home two or three nights later. After dinner with the family, we went to his study, where he showed me the *Fortune* issue. We spoke about what EVA might do for his company, and he further surprised me by asking me to address his board of directors the following Wednesday, at which time, he said, we would be hired. That was the fastest time in the history of our firm—five days—from meeting someone to being retained. Now, of course, if we had not met at the Henley dinner, Sussman might have sought me out. He could have telephoned me in New York. But the fact is that he took no action for months until we had that chance encounter. Little wonder that I tend to accept invitations. Since then, David and I have become close friends, and I am especially proud that he accepted my invitation to become a member of our International Advisory Board.

More often, the path to a client is far more circuitous. In 1996, we were implementing EVA at a firm called Cirrus Logic in San Jose, California. One day, the chairman invited me to address a meeting of an organization called TiE (The Indus Entrepreneur) on a Saturday morning at the Hyatt Hotel in San Jose. The chairman, himself from India, explained that the organization contained representatives from companies in the entire subcontinent—not only India but also Pakistan, Bangledesh, Sri Lanka, and Nepal. Prior to the TiE meeting, I was to be in Singapore for a few days; but I told my host that I would take an overnight flight to San Francisco and then drive to San Jose, arriving around noon the day before and giving me time to rest before the meeting. I neglected to ask him how many people would be there, but I figured no more than 25 would attend on a Saturday; and we sent out only that many packets of Stern Stewart material. I was astonished to find myself addressing 700.

The meeting went well; and afterward, I was approached by a man who said he represented the San Jose outpost of a federation of Indian companies called HCL. He was interested in installing an EVA program in his San Jose operation. I told him that I was of course interested, but that, from experience, I knew that the decision to adopt EVA would have to be made by his head office. Out of this conversation came an invitation to address a gathering of the HCL group in Delhi, India. The date was set for December 26, 1996. To assist in the presentation, I mobilized Mich Bergesen, then the head of our Johannesburg office, thereby truncating his Christmas holiday. But Mich has always been a good trouper. The session went well. I presented the rationale and overall design of an EVA program, after which Mich filled in the details of how an implementation worked. Within a few months, we won an assignment with one of the federation members, NIIT, one of the largest information technology companies in India.

After NIIT's EVA program started, I attended the steering committee meetings. It occurred to me that inasmuch as I was spending so much time in India I might as well do some more missionary work and make a few speeches. Around that time I ran into a man who headed the Morgan Stanley office in India. I interested him in our work and he eventually offered to have me give a presentation before some 75 CEOs of client companies of Morgan Stanley. (My persuasiveness was doubtless enhanced by the fact that his boss, Jack

Wadsworth, was a University of Chicago classmate and an old friend of mine. What a small world it is if you go to the right schools!) Out of these contacts came work for affiliates of Tata & Sons, as well as for another large Indian conglomerate, Godrej & Sons. Adi Godrej, after working closely with us, accepted my invitation to become a member of our International Advisory Board, as the sole representative of India.

We generated enough business in India so that in July 1999 we set up our office in Mumbai. All this resulted from a conference in far off Silicon Valley. And, oddly enough, we never did work for that HCL unit in California.

In selling our services, the ultimate pitch has to be made to the CEO. As I pointed out in the case of Fletcher Challenge in New Zealand, it bodes ill for our program if one persuades the board of directors and the chairman while the CEO remains skeptical. In over 30 years of selling, I have dealt with more than two thousand CEOs; and I think I've learned something about their sensibilities, their concerns, and—yes—their anxieties. They certainly deserve our sympathy. (After all, I'm one myself.) Corporate CEOs are inundated with so much information, so many new ideas, advice sensible and spurious, and nostrums of all sorts that they often remind me of astronomical bodies being pummelled by meteorite showers. It is easy to understand their wariness when another hotshot salesman appears. So how do you get their attention? How do you establish your credibility?

The answer is that you have to empathize with the conflicts and difficulties of being a CEO. You don't breeze in and immediately go into a sales pitch. In our case, we might open by saying, "It must be awfully frustrating that your stock price does not command anything like what you consider to be the fair value of the company." I would enlarge on the problem of trying to impress the market while avoiding gimmicks, or I would speak of the difficulties of motivating staff, words to this effect: "You get up in the morning and you think innovatively, imaginatively, creatively, from the time you awake until you get to the office; and then you continue to do so while you're in the office. What happens with middle-management people? What do they think about when they awake in the morning? They think about last night's ball score or what they're going to do this coming weekend. You do not reach these people; you do not influence their behavior. They are not motivated as you are, but there is something you can do about it. My EVA program addresses the problem directly."

I then segue into Stern Stewart's way of motivating people through incentives tied to performance; and before I finish, I've given an overview of our entire program. I also trot out the stories of companies that have had great success with EVA, such as SPX, Briggs & Stratton, Siemens AG, Herman Miller, and Metro AG, all of which I suggest would be happy to confirm my account. If I've initially gotten the CEO's attention, if I've broken through the meteorite shower, I get a full hearing. It is helpful, of course, if I'm dealing with a CEO who is intellectually curious. Not all are.

There are hazards, however, on the road to the sale, and you have to be quick at damage control. Greg Milano, a longtime partner who recently resigned to pursue other interests, has reminded me of the time in the early 1990s when we called on David Brink, one of the most respected and intellectually gifted South African executives, who heads Murray & Roberts, a large construction and construction engineering company outside of Johannesburg. I embarked on my standard pitch, on this occasion emphasizing what I was sure was Brink's dismay with managers who paid no heed to the balance sheet, squandered capital, were preoccupied solely with their own projects, and were past masters at negotiating bonuses involving targets that they could easily meet. As I ticked off this litany of frustrations, with Brink nodding and interspersing sardonic asides, I could see that he was warming to my approach. I had pushed his "hot buttons," in the graphic phrase whose origins escape me. We walked away with an assignment to do an EVA measurement study of the company.

About three months later, we were back to present our preliminary results to Brink and his team. The reaction was poor. A polite air of bafflement hung over the room. Brink finally spoke up to say, "You know, what you have presented is much too complicated for my people to understand." He clearly did not want to say that he himself had difficulty understanding it. Greg, who was an engineer by training and who was new with Stern Stewart, had in his innocence indulged his unrivaled talent for spinning complexities (he soon learned to simplify).

I was dismayed at Brink's reaction but quickly recovered to say, "We have failed you on this. There is a more simplified format we could have designed for you. I want you to give us another chance. We will do the exercise free of charge, and we will come back in six weeks and present it to you." We did so and landed the assignment. The presentation was one of Greg Milano's best.

On another occasion more recently, I was outlining our general approach to the CEO of a large Scandinavian company. As always, I emphasized the importance of our incentive bonus plan, arguing that its objectivity and long-term targets based on EVA achievements made it far superior to annually negotiated plans based largely on personal performance. The CEO heard me out and then told me that his wife had recently been informed by her employer that in future her compensation would include incentive pay dependent on performance. He said that she was "insulted" at the thought that she would do a better job if she was rewarded with more money. I was floored. I had never heard that complaint before, but I recovered to argue that an EVA implementation would always be designed to take account of cultural sensitivities in different countries. We would make it clear that incentive pay was not at odds with the work ethic but reinforced it. As I write, I still do not know whether we will get the assignment, but I think I made the only verbal recovery possible.

After getting the go-ahead comes the delicate job of negotiating our fee. With large companies, fees run into the millions; with small or medium-sized firms, fees are in the hundreds of thousands. But Stern Stewart does not bill on a time basis, like lawyers or accountants do. Candidly—and at the risk of sounding crass—I must say that we try to charge what the market will bear, based on the value we add to our clients. If we are going to create $300 million or $400 million of value for a medium-sized company and billions for a huge client, I want a reasonable share.

Clients generally accept the logic of our position, but bargaining with retail firms can be a problem. They think in terms of the immediate cost of the program and compare it to their net operating profit margin—say, 2 percent. Thus, if the proposed fee for a one-year implementation is $5 million, the head of a retail outfit may calculate that the companys' volume has to increase by $250 million to cover the cost of the program. It is an unsophisticated view, showing a dismaying ignorance of what EVA is all about. It is true, of course, that the $5 million fee has to be expensed in the year incurred, but it should be regarded as a long-term investment. And indeed, under EVA accounting, the fee is written off over the period of years when it is expected to have its impact, just as R&D is. Despite this misconception, we have served a number of retailers, including JC Penney, Toys R Us, Metro AG in Germany, Best Buy of Minneapolis, Whole Foods from Texas, New Clicks in Cape Town, and the aforementioned JD Group.

While clients in manufacturing or service industries do not have the retailer's hangup, they are still quite capable of complaining that the proposed fee is too high. I offer the stock argument that I put to the chap mentioned at the start of this chapter—a fee is neither abstractly high nor low, it depends on what your investment will yield—but my eloquence is not always persuasive. A few other gambits, however, are available. One is a "drop dead" clause. A company will contract for a full implementation that may take seven or eight months, or as much as three years, but with a clause in the contract that allows the client to cancel on 60 or 90 days' notice. The availability of this escape hatch is often the clinching argument.

Our willingness to take part of our fee in stock options, described at the end of Chapter 7, is also a useful bargaining tool. Not only does it underscore our belief in a favorable long-term outcome of the program, but it also appeals to (sadly) unsophisticated clients who believe that options cost them nothing (a subject that we discuss at length in Chapter 11). What is true, of course, is that an option grant as part of the fee reduces the immediate cash outlay, which can be important to a management strapped for cash.

Another approach to fee setting is to suggest a pilot program: let's take a division of the company, a discrete entity, and put it on EVA. See how it works out. If the experiment is successful, we can then extend it to the rest of the firm. And the fee may be only a tenth of what a full implementation would cost. If there is genuine interest on the part of the company, the offer is hard to resist.

If a pilot program is not possible, an alternative is an audit—a thorough study of the effectiveness of the value-enhancing activities of the firm, its strengths and deficiencies, a study that inevitably suggests that an EVA program would be more advantageous than present practices.

Stern Stewart can also offer a "familiarization study" as an alternative to a full-scale implementation or a pilot project. Generally lasting three or four months and typically costing $150,000 to $200,000, the study amounts to an extended tutorial in EVA measurement, incentive arrangements, and training programs, using the specific data of the client's operations rather than dealing with hypothetical examples. It is designed to give management a clear view of what it will be getting if it buys the full shebang. Both Diageo, the giant distilled-products company headquartered in London, and LaFarge, the French cement company, among others, went through the familiarization phase before signing up for the full program—acquiring a taste, as it were, before ordering the full meal.

But I don't want to give a false impression. Not infrequently, my arguments are unavailing. The prospect is just not buying. My eloquence brings no quickening response. If that were not the case, our business would be many times its present size. Nonetheless, we have been successful far beyond our first, ardent dreams. The point is that rejection is inherent in the selling process. I guess I learned that in my earliest days, when I was peddling decals. Not that I'm indifferent to rebuffs. They are painful, for a time. But I guess I have an inherent buoyancy of spirit that fills me with optimism as I approach a new prospect.

10

As for the Future

One of our great marketing advantages is that my colleagues and I have never had to sell a multiple-product line. The EVA methodology is adaptable to all manner of companies, large and small—every implementation is individually tailored— but EVA is still one product, relatively easy to describe in broad outline. Before EVA, we sold free cash flow as our major analytic tool to create shareholder wealth. By contrast, think of the marketing problems that confront a company with many products—say a book publisher, which issues several hundred books a year, each different. Recently, however, we have launched one new product and one new conceptual framework for which we entertain great hopes— BrandEconomics and the Wealth Added Index, both designed to respond to needs that had not been fully appreciated before.

A casual call from Stuart J. Agres to Al Ehrbar early in 1999 started the chain of events that led to BrandEconomics. Agres, the research director of the ad agency Young & Rubicam, was a national authority on the care and nurturing of brands, presiding over a vast database covering the brands of thousands of companies called BrandAsset Valuator (BAV). Agres had been looking for a correlation between the strength of brands and the financial performance of the companies that owned them. After examining several measures of financial performance, he found that the best correlations were with EVA and MVA—a near perfect fit.

Agres phoned Ehrbar with the thought that his findings might be of interest to us. Ehrbar, who was then in charge of our marketing, was indeed interested. After a meeting with Agres, he invited him to make a presentation to our partners. We listened attentively, but I'm chagrined to recall that we were quite skeptical about its relevance to our business. Nonetheless, we had no objection to Al's invitation to Agres to speak at the 1999 Senior Management Seminar, a three-day talkfest of the EVA Institute, held in March 1999 at the La Quinta resort near Palm Springs, California. For years it was our big annual event, attracting many prominent speakers (among them Nobel laureates Gary Becker, Myron Scholes, William Sharpe, the late Merton Miller, and management guru Peter Drucker) as well as Stern Stewart clients from around the world. Agres clearly wowed the crowd. From comments afterward, it was clear that his presentation was the most popular event at the session. That reaction led us to invite him for a return performance at a European seminar of the EVA Institute held in France in September of the same year.

By this time, the partners shared the enthusiasm of our clients and late in 1999 we began to talk with Young & Rubicam about a joint venture that would market the new product, BrandEconomics. The idea was to apply EVA analysis to the data in Y&R's BrandAsset Valuator to determine the economic value of specific brands in a company's portfolio. That had never been done before on an objective, empirical basis. All other methodologies for valuing brands are subjective, relying on "expert" opinion to quantify crucial variables. BAV had a wealth of information as to the strengths and weaknesses of brands and the reasons for these variations, but it could not put a dollar figure on its insights. What was attractive to us in the concept of BrandEconomics was not only that it was intellectually appealing but also that it could provide us with long-term relationships with clients, which occurred infrequently with EVA clients. An EVA implementation tended to be a one-shot deal, as I have mentioned before. The satisfied client sometimes brought us back for refresher training or for a reconfiguration of an incentive plan, but by and large the success of our business depended on the continual recruitment of new clients. On the other hand, the role of consultant to firms with many brands could result in a continuing relationship over many years, as clients sought advice on introducing new brands and retiring old ones.

In the summer of 2000, Mich Bergesen, who had been running the United Kingdom business in our London office, was transferred to New York to work on the detailed development of the new product, an assignment that occupied him for a year. As for the negotiations with Y&R, they had gone well for a time but came to a halt after the WPP Group began its acquisition of Y&R, as I explained in Chapter 8. After my conversation with Martin Sorrell on that Concorde flight, negotiations resumed but in the end, as I have said, we could not agree on the terms of a joint venture and instead entered into a four-year licensing agreement. Operations began in August 2001, with the formal launch of BrandEconomics LLC, a subsidiary of Stern Stewart, in February 2002. It is headed by Mich Bergesen and Al Ehrbar. The announcement of the firm's debut heralded "the first econometric model that calculates brand values based entirely on objective, observable data."

The methodologies of BrandAsset Valuator and EVA complement each other and indeed interlock. In analyzing the data in the BAV database, Y&R long ago discovered that the health and prosperity of brands is determined by four ingredients: differentiation, relevance, esteem, and knowledge. BAV calls them the "pillars of brand health." *Differentiation* is the quality that sets the brand apart from its competitors, that makes it unique, or at least special, enabling it to be priced at a premium. *Relevance* indicates the degree to which a brand is perceived to meet consumers' needs. (A great snow buggy, significantly different from its rivals, has little relevance in the tropics, and there is no market to be found among vegetarians for the tastiest hamburger patty.) *Esteem* relates to the reputation for quality and/or popularity that a brand evokes among consumers. *Knowledge* deals with the degree to which consumers are familiar with a brand.

A brand that is distinctive, highly relevant to the needs of many consumers who know it well and who hold it in high esteem is obviously a winner. The database, filled with responses from consumer surveys, tracks these four aspects and many other facets of thousands of brands, which wax and wane over periods of time. BAV bestows the term "leadership status" on those few brands—2 to 3 percent of all brands—that rank higher than the 80th percentile in each of the four pillars. Examples are Coca-Cola, Hallmark, and Microsoft. As a BrandEconomics brochure explains, "These brands have cultivated a tremendously powerful franchise with consumers, driving strong current performance while maintaining high future growth prospects. These brands also have great resilience to short-term business challenges or operational missteps."

The role of EVA is to quantify in monetary terms the value of a company's brands in the context of its business. An EVA analysis of a brand is no different than an analysis of a company, a division, or a branch office. In each case, EVA is of course the economic profit made after a deduction of a capital charge from net operating profit after tax (NOPAT), as readers of this volume are well aware by this time. With a brand, as well as with any other business unit to be measured, it is obviously necessary to know all its cost elements, its revenues, the amount of capital tied up in it, and, of course, the cost of the capital invested (equity as well as debt). Any return above the cost of capital—the minimum required by investors—obviously enhances the value of the brand.

The EVA analysis provides further enlightenment by separating the current EVA produced by a brand from its prospects for future growth. As the BrandEconomics brochure puts it, "Every intangible asset can be modeled, conceptually at least, in terms of these two components. Our brand framework explicitly looks at the Current Operations Value (COV) of a brand and its Future Growth Value (FGV). The COV measures the EVA produced by the brand in its current use and assumes that it continues into perpetuity with no growth. The FGV represents the EVA that could be realized both by growing the brand in existing markets . . . and by expanding the brand across new markets and categories."

The distinction between COV and FGV led to further insights as the data was explored. For most brands, Future Growth Value was found to be the largest part of their total value, whereas more mature and declining brands were more dependent on Current Operations Value. It was no great surprise that differentiation was usually the key element in brand success: "The higher a Brand's differentiation, the higher its current margin and future potential." Brands do even better that increase their relevance as well as their differentiation, showing "significant" increases in both margins and EVA.

This methodology provides the framework for BrandEconomics consultants to advise clients on the strategies they should employ in managing their brands. Having detailed information on the strengths and weaknesses of the client's brands, our people are able to suggest which brands to continue developing, which to simply milk, and which may be candidates for disposal.

One interesting assignment that landed in the BrandEconomics shop came from DuPont's textile and apparel divisons, which wanted to extend the reach of four of its brands into six new categories of products. The goal of the exercise was to determine which combination of brand and category would produce the best return on investment. Our people first studied the level of consumer acceptance of each brand-category combination—according to the four criteria, starting with differentiation—and then analyzed the likely economic impact. The most interesting conclusion was that the brand-category linkages that scored highest in potential sales were not necessarily the most profitable, due to different cost structures. Based on all this data, our team presented the client with its best-bet recommendations.

A different kind of assignment came from PacificCare Health Systems, based in Cypress, California, the largest regional health care provider in the United States. The company was planning to reposition its corporate brand. Before embarking on a major communications campaign, it wanted to understand two things: the degree of financial leverage that a strong brand would provide and the image attributes that would most effectively differentiate PacificCare from its competitors. BrandEconomics was hired to do a before-and-after study to benchmark the current health and profile of PacificCare's brand and those of twelve other health care providers operating in the western United States. Based on this research, we were able to demonstrate to PacificCare the strong relationship between brand strength and superior financial performance and to advise on the communications theme that would create a differentiated position for PacificCare in the marketplace. At the time of writing, our people were in the midst of the "after" study.

The Wealth Added Index (WAI), developed in our London office by Erik Stern and John Pigott, is not yet a product that we sell to customers (we hope it soon will be) but is a new concept and a new service we provide to the financial community, similar to the MVA rankings that we have published for years in the United States and several foreign countries. WAI grew out of the frustrations that Erik developed in recent years with the performance measure called Total Shareholder Return (TSR). It is a simple concept—the percentage rate of return from capital gains plus dividends. The term is used in the United States but is far more popular in Europe and throughout Asia.

Erik's frustration came from the observable fact that many companies that showed a positive TSR actually lost money for share-holders, in the same fashion that companies often show a gain in earnings per share while generating negative EVA, a subject we have discussed before. And for the same reason—in neither case is any calculation made for the cost of the equity furnished by investors. Simply put, the WAI calculation starts with the TSR figure and deducts from it the cost of equity capital multiplied by the opening market value of equity (share price times the number of shares) for the given period. The cost of capital varies, of course, depending on the relative risk in the business; the greater the risk, the higher the rate of return required by investors. Moreover, for any given period, WAI takes into account not only the opening equity capital figure but also insertions of new equity during the period, generally for acquisitions. The calculation is made each day when dividends or new shares are issued, the numbers coming from a service called Thomson Financial Datastream.

In a monograph on the subject written by Stern and Pigott, the authors deal with what they call the Vodafone Paradox:

> Vodafone chalked up a high TSR over five years—a whopping 248%—even though it overpaid for acquisitions and licenses. However, over parts of the period, many sharehold-ers experienced negative TSR—their shares were worth less than when they bought them. . . . Vodafone's EVA kept falling, even as its EBITDA, or earnings before interest, taxes, depreciation, and amortization, rose. In other words, how could a company which does so badly in terms of value creation turn in such a great TSR? What measure would truly reflect its value-destroying performance? The answer: one that included all investors' shareholdings over the period, benchmarked against the cost of equity. Wealth Added analysis . . . revealed startling wealth destruction. Most of the

$145 billion or so lost between 1996 and [June] 2001 was sacrificed to Vodafone's bids for third-generation [cell phone] licenses and to acquire its German counterpart, Mannesmann.

In my opinion, that harsh view of Stern and Pigott was validated by the 2002 Global WAI Ranking that covered 100 companies over the five-year period ending in December 2001. The ranking placed Vodafone Airtouch PLC at the tail end of the Bottom 50, closely followed by three other telecommunications companies. Many other celebrated companies were in negative territory, among them Coca-Cola, AOL Time Warner, Disney, Compaq Computer, Deutsche Telecom, Mitsubishi Heavy Industries, and the Boeing Company. Wal-Mart Stores headed the Top 50, with $149.6 billion in wealth added, followed by Microsoft with $93.8 billion and IBM with $93.1 billion.

WAI's debut in print was under illustrious auspices. The *Economist* was the launchpad for the first list, published in its December 1, 2001, issue, which covered the period 1996 to June 2001, followed by the *Financial Times* on October 9, 2002, with the global ranking. "SEARCH FOR AN INDEX THAT CAN BE COUNTED ON," headlined the *FT*. "A string of corporate disasters has increased the demand among investors for better ways to monitor the worth of their shareholdings." Lists were also published in newspapers in Denmark, Finland, France, the Netherlands, Norway, Portugal, Spain, and Sweden.

Early in 2003, Erik Stern and John Pigott published another monograph introducing a companion program to WAI, Relative Wealth Added (RWA). It made its journalistic debut in a laudatory article in the *Sunday Times* of London on January 26. Simply put, RWA compares the wealth added by a particular company with the record of its peer group. It is an excellent guide to managerial performance, so long as the peer group is accurately selected, for such comparisons screen out the impact of general economic conditions as well as the effects of booms and busts in the stock market.

I regard WAI as the third generation of value-based metrics that Stern Stewart has contributed. First came free cash flow, then EVA and MVA, which we have discussed at length, and now WAI and RWA. WAI has certain advantages over MVA. MVA does not take into account the cost of capital; it is simply market capitalization minus the company's economic book value. Moreover, to derive economic book value, one must make a number of adjustments to the accounting figures that are available, such as capitalizing R&D and advertising costs and writing these off over a period of years. Making these adjustments from publicly available data produces only a relatively rough approximation of the true situation. It still tells a lot, but WAI, by contrast, does not have to deal with accounting data at all. It is thus able to generate global comparisons, which MVA cannot do because accounting rules vary greatly from country to country.

WAI and RWA have the additional advantage of being measures that can tie incentive-compensation systems directly to wealth creation. That occurs with EVA bonuses, too, of course. But, as Stern and Pigott reason in their paper on WAI:

> EVA motivates managers to deliver today and, in a well-designed incentive scheme, over the medium term. Wealth Added encourages them to balance performance today and building capabilities for the medium and longer term. The measures complement each other. . . . If a manager has "clear line of sight" to the share price, then Wealth Added is appropriate. . . . In cases where the share price seems remote and beyond influence, then EVA will be the most appropriate measure.

For senior management, Stern and Pigott suggest incentive plans based on both WAI and EVA and based on EVA alone further down the line. In their monograph on RWA, they add another suggestion—that RWA be used in devising short-term incentive plans for top management. We have not yet developed new bonus plans based on these performance measures—at which point they will become new products—but our people are always at the drawing board. Our business has always been an exciting intellectual adventure. It will remain so as far as I can see into the future.

11

The Credo of a Radical Free Marketeer

O ne of the incidental pleasures of lecturing is entertaining questions from the audience, often a lot of questions— some frivolous, a few hostile, but mostly questions of serious intent. As I travel from country to country, there is also the odd TV appearance and press interview, with more questions. Like other foreign visitors, I feel flattered by the notion that my views are of heightened significance because of their distant origin. The questions themselves cover all sorts of subjects. Some involve technical issues of financial theory, others the vast scope of corporate governance; still others deal with fundamental philosophic issues, such as the appropriate role of government in the economy and society as a whole. Throughout 2002 and 2003, the spate of business scandals, starting with the Enron case in 2001, generated an endless series of questions about the causes of corporate crime and what can be done to prevent it, or at least to limit its incidence.

I propose to respond here to these frequently asked questions, but before doing so I should describe my general approach. As the reader may remember from my first encounter with the work of

Milton Friedman, and later with that of George Stigler and Merton Miller, I am a libertarian to the core—a believer in markets and thus strongly of the view that prices and fluctuations in prices provide suppliers and consumers with invaluable information. I also believe fervently in the desirability of limited government, especially on the federal level, as limited as is practical for a large nation that requires a massive defense establishment, a national police force (actually several), and a bureaucracy to collect taxes (even with a flat tax, an agency like the Internal Revenue Service would still be necessary, but with the simple role of enforcement, not massive negotiations). We also would need a judicial structure to decide contractual disputes and to enforce the rule of law. Compared to the rest of the government, the legislative establishment is not large.

What parts of government would I get rid of? The entire welfare state, with all its income-transfer programs. A breathtaking prospect, no? Yes indeed, but I am speaking of an ideal. If the welfare state were to be abolished, piece by piece, there would have to be extended periods of transition to honor claims already contracted for, such as redistributed income to the elderly. It would be unfair, as well as politically impossible, to betray the expectations of people who have based their plans for the future on a set of economic arrangements established for well over half a century. There is an implied social contract between government and the governed that cannot be abruptly terminated, but only gradually revised.

But why do libertarians want to revise these economic arrangements? Basically because they create as many problems as they try to solve, if not more—undesirable and harmful disincentives. There are secondary and tertiary effects of government action that are not foreseen—the famous unanticipated consequences that the late Senator Daniel Patrick Moynihan did so much to publicize. Raising the minimum wage will help low-wage workers who retain their jobs, but it does not help those who lose their jobs because employers cannot afford the higher wage bill. Unemployment compensation, designed to tide workers over until they find work, has the paradoxical effect of acting as a disincentive to unemployed workers at the margin—the millions who can only command modest wages and who see no reason to seek work while they collect almost as much on the dole, given that they are spared the cost of transportation and, in many instances, taxes. Subsidizing sugar production through import quotas helps a small group of producers but raises the prices for everyone who consumes sugar. There are many more examples. Beyond the basic economic issues is the fundamental concern I have with the loss of individual liberty, one of our most precious possessions. And so to the questions, in no particular order.

Question 1.   We hear a lot these days about greed as the root cause of the corporate scandals that fill the headlines. Alan Greenspan, for one, has coined the term "infectious greed," arguing that "It is not that humans have become any more greedy than in generations past," but that "the venues to express greed had grown so enormously." What do you make of this? Is greed the cause of the shocking behavior that roiled the markets in 2002?

Answer.   Not necessarily. First of all, what happened at Enron, WorldCom, Adelphia, and the others was outrageous. The culprits should be punished severely and some are likely to go to prison. But the term *greed* is tossed around too loosely and is often applied indiscriminately to the successful and the affluent. The truth is that greed is not a useful term to explain economic phenomena or the reward structure in our society. The dictionary definition of *greed* is an excessive craving for more than one needs. A glutton can be greedy for food, an affluent clothes horse can covet half the inventory of Bergdorf Goodman, Mrs. Marcos reputedly amassed 3,000 pairs of shoes. Some people can be both greedy and miserly. Greedy is a psychological term, which can only be applied fairly by one who knows enough about the individual concerned. It is quite possible, of course, that the corporate scoundrels whose exploits shocked the nation were animated by greed. Their jailhouse memoirs may tell the tale.

Moreover, one cannot equate greed with any specific sum of money. There was a time in our history when newsboys aspired to become millionaires, which to generations brought up on Horatio Alger did not seem to be a greedy ambition. The depreciation of the dollar over the years has made that much too modest a goal. One can almost say that millionaires are now a dime a dozen. So where is the cutoff point for greed—$10 million, $15 million, $100 million? It's an absurd question that admits of no answer. The absurdity is underscored by the fact that business success is calibrated in money, which is not the case with artists, writers, teachers, the clergy, or almost any other member of the liberal professions.

It is sad, however, that the word *greed* is frequently bandied about to denigrate people who earn large sums of money, particularly top corporate executives. The revelation, in a proxy statement, that a CEO earned $20 million or $30 million or $40 million in a year is taken as proof positive that the executive suite is awash in greed. This is nonsense. Curiously, the same charge is not as frequently leveled at movie stars who get $20 million for a picture or athletes with multiyear contracts that guarantee them a fortune once they sign. Why this indulgence? An often-heard explanation is that movie stars and athletes have a relatively short working life. But the tenure of CEOs is often equally brief, either because most are appointed within 10 years of retirement or because of failure. The long tenure of a Jack Welch is not typical.

Market forces are also invoked in behalf of actors and athletes: The stars bring in big box office, hence there is competition for their services and thus the high prices they command. But there is similar competition for the services of corporate stars or potential stars, particularly on the upswing of the business cycle. CEOs and boards are always worried about the problem of "retention"—by which they mean losing talented staff who are seduced by better offers elsewhere. The true explanation for the dichotomy in attitudes is probably that the public idolizes movie stars and athletes (and identifies with them in fantasy) while it has an animus toward businesspeople that is deeply rooted in our long populist tradition.

In its September 2, 2002, issue *Fortune* published a cover story with the title "You Bought. They Sold." The subtitle read, "Since 1999 hundreds of greedy execs at America's worst-performing companies have sold $66 billion worth of stock." Six executives who did particularly well, realizing from $475 million to $1.57 billion, had their pictures on the cover, including the chairman of AOL Time Warner, which owns *Fortune*. There were many more pictures on the inside pages, with capsule accounts of the huge sums realized by stock sales. There were no data on the cost of the shares, but *Fortune* was doubtless correct that the cost was relatively modest. But what had made these individuals "greedy"? Simply the fact that they had cleaned up. They sold when their shares were priced high, before the bubble burst. (Most of the shares sold, needless to say, were of high-tech companies.) But what was wrong with cleaning up? The article stated, "In some cases insiders clearly cheated the investment community to realize their gains—by ginning up revenue numbers that have turned out to be phony." The article, however, gave only two examples of revised figures. Clearly, it was appropriate for *Fortune* to denounce fraud, if that occurred—it was hardly proven—but *Fortune's* main criticism was that it was unfair and greedy for insiders to cash out at the top of the boom while less sophisticated investors were at the buying end. One gathers that the ethical thing would have been for insiders to watch passively as their shares declined in value, as did a couple of executives mentioned in the story. It was certainly better public relations.

But let us be fair. There are unexceptional reasons for corporate insiders to sell. For one thing, when anyone exercises an option, income tax has to be paid. Anyone in the top tax brackets, federal and state, might have to sell nearly half of his or her shares just to pay tax. Second, a top executive who sold some holdings at a high price might just have followed the prudent practice of diversifying. Third, the executive might also have had a realistic appreciation of just how inflated share prices had become at the height of the market boom and decided to profit from that fact. What's corrupt about that?

But weren't compensation committees and boards of directors spectacularly generous in bestowing option grants on executives? In some cases yes, but not always. When many companies issued options, it was with the expectation or at least the hope of a moderate rise in share prices over the next few years. Instead, toward the end of the 1990s, the market went wild: share prices for the dot-coms and other hot companies soared and option holders were enriched beyond their dreams. In other cases, it is true that many boards are in the pockets of the chief executive. They are anything but independent and a process of mutual enrichment goes on at the expense of the shareholder.

What is intolerable—and illegal—are sales by insiders prompted by inside information of which the public is ignorant. It is not an uncommon phenomenon and it occasionally produces a big enforcement action. But *Fortune* did not make that charge.

Question 2.   But what is wrong with trading on inside information? Doesn't it promote market efficiency, as many professors of finance maintain?

Answer.   It is true that the gradual filtering of inside information into the markets, through trades, promotes efficiency, by which we mean that prices more accurately come to reflect the real condition of a firm. This effect is less significant, incidentally, if a blockbuster piece of information is about to burst over the market that will devastate a company's shares or if favorable news will send the price soaring. An example would be a pharmaceutical company whose top management suddenly discovers that it is about to be denied Food and Drug Administration approval of a new drug or that the FDA is requiring that a profitable drug be withdrawn. In such a case, if a few individuals are tipped off and trade a day or two before the news is announced, the effect of their trading—unless it is enormous—is likely to be far outweighed by the spectacular impact of the news itself when it is announced.

Even when market efficiency results from trading on inside information, it violates every sense of fairness. We are not dealing here with a victimless crime, as frequently stated. Though nameless and faceless to the inside trader, there are real victims—the people on the other side of the illicit transaction. An inside trader who buys victimizes the unseen seller who lacks the crucial information. Similarly, someone who sells because of an inside tip victimizes the ignorant buyer. It is a zero-sum game. That reality would be even clearer if the trade were made not on a stock exchange but between two people sitting across a table.

Proposals to legalize insider trading place a much greater value on the efficiency of markets than I do. Such a move would only reinforce the cynicism and the distrust about the markets caused by the deluge of corporate scandals. In his book, *Shady Business: Confronting Corporate Corruption*, Irwin Ross, my collaborator, wrote: "If insider trading were legalized, the proverbial playing field would become so tilted as to break into two tiers: one for the professionals with access to inside dope and the other for the untutored mass of players. One can imagine the shock and disillusion and the exodus from the market. Moreover, among the professionals, bribery in the pursuit of inside information would become rampant."

There would be many more Dennis Levines and Ivan Boeskys, but this time they would not go to jail. Remember those names from the 1980s? Levine, a hotshot mergers-and-acquisitions specialist with a string of tipsters in different investment banks, made a small fortune in illegal trades over a seven-year period, largely through advance knowledge of M&A deals. He covered his tracks by having his trades made by offshore banks. Levine, in turn, was a tipster for

Ivan Boesky, who paid him a percentage of his winnings. Boesky at the time was a celebrated arbitrageur, who wrote a widely reviewed book on the subject. Only after his arrest did the world learn how unorthodox his methods were. If their activities had been legal, both Levine and Boesky would have become role models rather than jail birds.

Question 3. How do you account for the recent deluge of corporate scandals and what can be done to prevent a recurrence?

Answer. The sheer number of scandals has certainly focused our attention, but it is worth remembering that egregious corporate misbehavior has long been with us. A bit of historical perspective might be useful. Imagine the headlines today that would greet the news that the head of the New York Stock Exchange had embezzled funds entrusted to him by his brokerage customers and was being packed off to jail. That occurred in 1938, when Richard Whitney, eminent socialite, was sent up the river. Or imagine the shocked disbelief that would greet the news that a construction company had bribed scads of congressmen and other Washington dignitaries to prevent an investigation of its affairs. That's exactly what happened in 1872, when an indiscreet letter was published that was written by Oakes Ames, a Massachusetts congressman who headed the Credit Mobilier railroad construction company. The bribes took the form of shares in Credit Mobilier—the shares were given as gifts or were sold at par, far below their market value—and nobody went to jail. Nothing like that happens today.

The dollar volume of recent scandals seems greater than anything in the past, but not after one does the inflation adjustment. After the suicide in March 1932 of Ivar Kreuger, the famous Swedish "match king," investigators found that he "had inflated earnings on the books of his various real and unreal companies by more than a quarter of a billion dollars" during the period 1917–1932, according to Robert Shaplen's biography, *Kreuger, Genius and Swindler*. He was a genius at creating phony assets, among them $120 million in counterfeit Italian government bonds. Apply the inflation multiple, and you get within the range of the Enron and WorldCom and other telecoms' bookkeeping hijinks.

Boom times generate excesses and when the boom collapses the scandals emerge. That was the case in the 1920s, and that is the case today. In the roaring twenties, long before the Securities and Exchange Commission was created, probably the most popular scam was the "pool." It involved concerted action by pool operators to buy and sell the shares of a company to draw in the public, artificially inflating the share price, and then "pulling the plug" by selling out, gradually, so that the price would not collapse all at once. The pool operators, who had bought shares when the price was low, would clean up; and the "greater fools," who had been sucked in during the upswing, would lose. A later Senate investigation found that in 1929, the shares of 105 corporations had been the targets of pools—among them some of the best-known U.S. companies, such as American Tobacco, Bethlehem Steel, Chrysler, Continental Can, R. H. Macy, Monsanto Chemical, and U.S. Rubber.

Insiders often participated in the pools, feeding information to the pool operators that helped them stir up market interest by floating rumors and newspaper stories. A pool involving the stock of the Chase National Bank made nearly $1.5 million in less than four months in 1929. The bank participated in the pool, as did its chairman, Albert H. Wiggin. The Chase Securities Corporation, Chase's investment banking affiliate, took part in eight pools in its own stock in a four-year period ending in July 1931. The biggest shocker involving Chase was Wiggin's profit of $4 million made by shorting his own stock in September 1929, a month before the market crash that sent Chase's shares plunging. There is no reason to believe that Wiggin anticipated the crash, but the conflict of interest involved in a top executive betting on the decline of his own company's shares is, well, breathtaking. And people were truly shocked at the time.

Wiggin felt compelled to give up the $100,000-a-year pension that his fellow directors had bestowed on him when he retired. In that crazy era, however, he had done nothing illegal.

It might have been anticipated, but wasn't, that the boom years of the 1990s would incubate their own species of scandal. On the whole the deceits were more sophisticated than those in the 1920s. The big cases did not involve rigging the market—pools had been outlawed by the SEC—but manipulating the books to inflate earnings and support share prices. "Managing earnings" in a perfectly legal way, such as trade loading and juggling reserve accounts, has long been an art form in American corporations, as previously discussed. But in recent years, financial legerdemain had become more deft, bookkeeping had become more "creative," and derivatives ushered in an era of new and arcane financial instruments that made it easier to cover up. Something called "structured banking" enabled the financial wizards at Enron to create intricate partnerships to remove debt from the balance sheet and thus to maintain its credit rating and bank borrowings. It was a jerry-built structure and it finally collapsed, but not before insiders enriched themselves.

At WorldCom, the sleight of hand was simpler and bolder—loading the balance sheet with billions of dollars of current expenses, thereby prettying up the profit-and-loss statement and bolstering profits. All went well until a new management felt compelled to reveal the truth and take the company into bankruptcy. At the time of writing, there have been four guilty pleas by top executives at WorldCom and two at Enron.

As always, boom times in the 1990s generated a giddiness, a willingness to take desperate gambles, a lack of restraint and (it would seem) a pathological inability to recognize the personal hazards in skirting the law. I used to think that a regard for personal reputation would restrain any delinquency in the executive suite. I thought everyone would prize a good name above all else, for without the esteem of one's fellows, without a reputation for honesty and integrity, how could one succeed in the long run or, indeed, have any self-esteem? Well, I was wrong. Clearly, for many people the pursuit of easy riches made them heedless of any other concern.

So what can be done to prevent a recurrence of these scandals? As suggested earlier, I would throw the book at the guilty. No matter what the case is with street criminals, jail time is a powerful deterrent to white-collar crime. There is no reason to worry about recidivism with these offenders, for it is hard to believe that any of them will ever hold a top job again in a large corporation; the whole point of substantial jail terms and heavy fines is to deter other financial hotshots who might be tempted in the future. There is nothing like long prison sentences and perhaps multi-million-dollar fines to drive the lesson home.

The markets, of course, quickly imposed automatic penalties by deep-sixing the share prices of offending corporations. Board members who were indifferent to fiduciary responsibilities (or are so suspected) have been hit by multi-million-dollar class action law suits that will take years to resolve. This is no more than simple justice—and it should act as a powerful warning to other outside directors who regard board membership as no more than a sinecure. Top executives who bailed out with fortunes before their high-flying companies collapsed face the same legal challenges. Even if they escape conviction and retain part of their hoard after settling claims, they will have gone through hell and will remain pariahs in their communities. Their plight should also act as a deterrent to would-be imitators.

If I had my druthers, I would have left matters to the reflexive actions of the marketplace and to the self-imposed reforms of boards of directors that have been educated the hard way. But if they see a problem, most Americans like to pass a law and so in August 2002, Congress passed and the president signed the Sarbanes-Oxley Act, which tightened the reporting requirements of public companies, ended certain practices that were subject to abuse, and placed the accounting profession under a new supervisory board. Some provisions may be helpful in preventing future fraud, although the full effect of any legislation usually cannot be known for years; and there may well be deleterious consequences that were never anticipated—which is why I am always leery of new laws, however well-intentioned. To promote transparency, the Sarbanes-Oxley Act provides that corporate insiders report trades in their company's shares by the end of the second day after the transaction, which does seem a clear gain over the much longer period previously allowed. CEOs and CFOs must now attest personally to the accuracy of periodic financial reports. A false certification, made knowingly, can subject the culprit to a jail term of up to 20 years (which will doubtless concentrate attention but does seem more than a bit of overkill).

At the same time, the act increases maximum penalties for wire and mail fraud, the standard charges in securities fraud cases, from 5 years to 10 years. Another punitive provision applies to financial restatements resulting from misconduct, which triggers disgorgement of CEO and CFO bonuses and profits from stock sales, if criminal intent is proven. Private litigants in securities law cases are also benefited by extending the statute of limitations; a suit now can be brought up to five years after the violation, or two years after its discovery, whichever is earlier. Among its other provisions, the act also outlaws loans to corporate officers and board members—a great area of abuse in the past, when companies made loans at below-market rates of interest to favored colleagues and then often forgave them. Such loans are allowed if the company is in the business of making consumer loans or issuing credit cards. But in their zeal to curb an abuse, the lawmakers overlooked other legitimate reasons to make loans, such as the need to help a recruit buy a house in a hot real estate market like Silicon Valley. Without the sweetener, the recruit might reject the job offer.

The new law does not deal at all with a major problem in the investment banking industry—the conflict of interest between securities analysts and the bankers. When I first got into the finance business, analysts and investment bankers kept their distance from each other. There was not precisely a Chinese wall between them, but analysts were compensated on the basis of the acuity of their research reports, the accuracy of their forecasts, and the following they developed (which meant sales) among customers. It was well-known that their employer and the analysts themselves might have positions in the stocks they recommended, but there was no conflict of interest because a statement to that effect was printed on every research report. In the great boom of the 1990s, many an analyst became an arm of the investment bankers, tailoring "research" to attract underwriting business to the firm and being compensated in large part on the degree of his or her success.

I had a personal experience along these lines a few years ago when we were thinking of taking Stern Stewart public. An official of one investment bank, in urging us to come with his firm, pointed out that "We have an analyst who follows companies like yours." That was all, but I was innocent enough to be shocked. "You mean that if you handle our IPO," said I, "the analyst will give us favorable write-ups?" Even more interesting was the implication that if we did not hire that firm, the analyst would not follow us or recommend us. The banker said no more, but in the end we decided not to go public.

Since the scandals broke, the debasement of the research analyst's function has generated a lot of publicity. Nobody defends the derelictions, and there is no need really for a law to outlaw it. Market pressure can bring reform; for without it, research reports will not be worth the paper they are written on.

While I am generally leery of regulations, because of their unintended consequences, I make exceptions for those that favor transparency. One regulation that I propose would require all members of boards of directors to file annually a list of their holdings with the SEC. That would enable shareholders and the press to spot conflicts of interest before they create embarrassment or worse.

Question 4.   The mass distribution of stock options in recent years has generated enormous controversy. Where do you stand on the various issues?

Answer.   Options provide a useful incentive for executives who are in a position to affect the overall direction of a company and thus its share price. But options are of far less value when distributed down the line to employees who can only influence the unit or the operation where they work. For such employees, bonuses based on EVA improvement in their bailiwicks offer a far better incentive.

Options have their drawbacks, not to say abuses. When most options are granted, the exercise price is usually set at the market price. That frequently guarantees a profit in a rising market, without top management having done anything to improve performance. Around 75 percent of share-price movements are due not to the performance of management but to either broad movements in the stock market or conditions that are industry specific. This makes options a blunt instrument as a management incentive. Moreover, the period before the option can be exercised is often too short, which gives top management a perverse incentive to manipulate earnings to inflate the share price in the short run, often to the detriment of the firm's long-term prospects.

There is a way, of course, to avoid these pitfalls. An option can be designed with a rising exercise price, year by year—basically rising in tandem with the firm's cost of capital. The details get complicated (they are spelled out in *The EVA Challenge*, pp. 152–154), but the essential point is that the "steadily rising exercise price is designed to ensure that, if the stock price does not produce at least a cost-of-capital return for the option period, the options are worthless. Thus, executives cannot benefit unless shareholders receive the minimum return on their investment to which they are entitled." If the company's performance is above the threshold, executives can benefit handsomely.

This type of option, which Stern Stewart has been advocating for years and which was originated by Bennett Stewart, clearly aligns the interests of managers with those of shareholders. But I would go further by granting these options to outside directors on corporate boards, in lieu of the fees they now receive—or at least partly so. I know this is a radical proposal, but I can think of no better way to ensure that independent directors are fixated on the long-term future of the corporations they serve.

A basic reform of the entire options system, much debated of late, would require public companies to record option grants as a current expense, just like any other form of compensation. It has long been one of the most absurd accounting fictions that options are cost free. It is recognized, of course, that options when exercised dilute ownership; and companies routinely report earnings on a fully diluted basis (though they don't highlight the calculation in annual reports). But the notion that options are a freebie because they do not involve cash outlays is belied by the fact that if companies sell options (such as warrants), they certainly get money for them. And if they issue options on stock that has been returned to the corporate treasury through a buy-back program, the cash value of the option grant is quite clear. It is true that there are technical problems in putting a price on the value of options. The Black-Scholes option-pricing model, commonly used for options of shorter duration, needs to be modified; but these technical difficulties are not insurmountable.

So why the resistance to recording the cost of options? It is largely because of the huge option grants given by high-tech companies, which have lobbied strenuously against the change when it has been proposed. The high-tech companies have long been profligate with options in justifying modest salaries, and they fear that reporting the cost of options would depress their profits or wipe them out entirely, thereby sinking their share prices. This fear proves how financially unsophisticated many corporate leaders are. The truth is that the markets are sufficiently efficient to take into account the effect of these option grants; a small army of securities analysts ferret out every last detail. The anxiety about expensing options is similar to the fear many executives expressed back in the mid-1970s when the accountants decided to treat R&D as an ordinary business expense rather than writing it off gradually over its expected future economic life. Earnings per share declined, but the practice had no noticeable impact on share prices. The analysts were well aware that R&D was already being expensed on corporate tax returns. Most companies do not face the presumed option problem to the same extent as the high-tech sector does. Corporate sentiment was also changing in 2002 as a result of all the scandals. Coca-Cola and a few other large companies announced that they were now going to report the cost of options, and there may be a bandwagon effect. Naysayers warn that if the accounting rules change, fewer options may be issued in the future. This is extremely doubtful.

Question 5.   The uproar over corporate corruption has been accompanied by strenuous criticism of the stratospheric sums paid to chief executives in recent years. An article in *The American Prospect*, for example, states that "In 1999, the average chief executive earned 419 times more than his or her co-workers, up from 25 times in 1981, while the 10 highest-paid executives have seen their income soar an astonishing 4,300 percent between 1981 and 2000." Is this something to be concerned about, or is it part of the same old blather about greed?

Answer.   It is obviously a source of concern—especially because of the populist criticism from left-leaning pundits and politicians—if high-priced corporate stars do not perform for the shareholders. And that's clearly often been the case, not only in the scandal-tarred companies like Enron and WorldCom but also in such old-line companies as AT&T. But what to do about it? Clearly, not pass a law, as was done in 1993, at the urging of the Clinton administration. There was an outcry then about sky-high executive pay, and the Clintons responded by getting a law passed disallowing the deductibility of compensation above $1 million, unless it was tied to performance. This resulted in fewer bonuses, for which were substituted grants of stock and a deluge of stock options, all technically linked to performance.

In fact, almost all managements that received large option gains did so unexpectedly. The gains were an accident. First, the Clintons' 1993 tax-law change that had a performance test on compensation above $1 million necessarily led compensation committees of boards of directors to use options to meet the performance test; but little did anyone know that share prices would rise an average of 25 to 30 percent a year, three times the historical average. Since options are three times riskier than cash, an intended $1 million cash bonus translated into an average of $3 million in options; but the options generated three times this figure on average from 1994 to 2000. Thus $1 million a year from 1994 through 1999, a total of $6 million (subject to income tax of 50 percent and thus worth $3 million), converts to option gains of approximately $60 million before tax, a multiple of 20.

Today the problem is likely to be self-correcting to some degree. The bear market blowoff in the 2000–2002 period has taken the bloom off options—the largest component of those hefty pay packets—and a new concern for public opinion, a new sensitivity to those charges of greed, is now becoming apparent in many of our largest corporations. A self-imposed restraint is likely to prevail for a time—at least until the markets go wild again. Then we may have a recurrence of the problem.

Question 6. Most business schools offer courses on ethics and, since the scandals broke, have given them considerable publicity. Even President Bush, a Harvard MBA, has urged that "Our schools of business must be principled teachers of right and wrong and not surrender to moral confusion and relativism." Do you think that greater emphasis on teaching ethics will change behavior for the better and help prevent a recurrence of the scandals?

Answer.   I doubt it. Right and wrong must be taught at home and must take hold at any early age. Ethical dilemmas can be dealt with in business school classes, and they make for some fascinating discussions—such as relations between salesmen and buyers, how much entertainment can be proferred by a salesman without stepping over the line, or proper tactics in a negotiation, how good is a handshake if you get a better offer, the conflict between group loyalty and the moral imperative to be a whistle blower, and so on. But the scandals that dominated the headlines did not pivot on the fine points of ethical behavior. They involved allegations of outright fraud (Enron and WorldCom), theft from corporate coffers (Enron and Adelphia), tax evasion (Denis Koslowski and the unpaid sales tax on those paintings), and blatant coverups (document shredding at Arthur Andersen). No ethical dilemmas here, little substance for classroom argument.

What are useful are classes in business law, including the techniques of law enforcement agencies. This may be cynical, but there conceivably might be less crime if hotshot students learned how vulnerable nonprofessional criminals are to detection and if the students are shown that when laws are broken punishment is severe, swift, and certain.

Question 7.   In some of your statements, you have spoken favorably of certain actions of government. How does that square with your libertarian principles? Overall, what do you regard as the appropriate role of government?

Answer.   I see no contradiction in favoring the use of the government's police power against white-collar crime, which is what much of the corporate scandals come down to. But let's talk first of general principles. What is the proper role of government? Some years ago, in that hilarious satirical BBC series called *Yes, Minister*, the top civil servant in the mythical Department of Administrative Affairs told the minister that government had no concern with morality; its sole job was to maintain order, avoid chaos. Over the centuries, that cynical view probably reflected reality. But in a democracy, the role of government clearly is to protect personal liberty, which means not only First Amendment rights but also, of equal importance, the right to acquire and dispose of property. Without private property, the state becomes all powerful and individuals have little or no defense against it. Moreover, it is not just liberty that needs protecting. Individuals must protect themselves against the perverse incentives that government generates, often in the name of desirable goals. I've already mentioned the disincentive effects of minimum wage laws and unemployment compensation. Affirmative action presents similar problems, to which we will come later.

How far do we take individual freedom? You remember the old saw that the freedom to move my fist is limited by the proximity of your chin? People do not always heed that limitation, and therefore we need a judicial system, we need police protection, and we need a national defense system to protect all of us. But we don't require the lion's share of what government currently provides, on both the national and the local level. Moreover, to the extent that government services are deemed necessary, they should be provided locally if at all possible. Diversity removes the curse of uniformity, allows innovation; and local option also allows individuals in many cases to opt out by moving to another community, which is easier than moving to another country.

Question 8.   What services would you have government eliminate?
    Answer.   A great many. I would get rid of farm subsidies, export subsidies, and import restrictions, which of course are a subsidy to domestic producers at the expense of the consumer. I would privatize, or partially privatize, many government activities, from the social security system to—yes—the public school system. One of the guiding principles in all this is that if an activity is deemed essential by the electorate, it can often be mandated by government but does

not necessarily have to be financed and owned by government. A good example is compulsory automobile insurance, with the car owner being free to buy it wherever it is available.

None of the changes that I favor would be abrupt. As I suggested earlier, it would be morally outrageous (as well as politically impossible) to sunder the implied social contract between government and the governed in many areas of life. Take social security. I believe it was an error to establish the system back in 1935. It was clearly an infringement of individual liberty to tax people to contribute to a government savings plan for their old age. But the country has lived with this system for nearly 70 years. Any reform in that area would have to guarantee the pensions of the millions of current retirees and of those close to retirement under the present regulations. For them the system would not change.

For the others, I would invoke the principle previously described of a government mandate of private activity—in this case, a compulsory savings program run not by government but by the individual beneficiaries. New entrants to the labor force could be compelled to set up individual retirement accounts into which they would deposit a stipulated percentage of income. They would have total control of their funds and could invest in equities, corporate or government bonds, mutual funds, or any combination that they wished. But what about the millions of individuals not close to retirement who had already accumulated social security credits? Under my plan, control of these funds would be transferred to the beneficiaries, after which they would make their annual contributions. When they will be ready for retirement, they should be far better off than current retirees, whose pensions are limited by formulas based on past income. Studies have shown that broadly diversified equity portfolios, built up over the decades, would have substantially higher returns—despite all the market volatility—than the relatively modest pensions that retirees now collect.

I am also concerned that some disadvantaged people contribute to retirement programs without ever receiving benefits because their life expectancy is significantly lower than that of the more economically fortunate. This is one of the examples of unintended discrimination in our country.

Question 9.   You want to get government out of education. Why? And how would you do it?

Answer.   I grant you that this is perhaps my boldest proposal. The "why" is the easiest to deal with. The public school system, particularly in our large cities, has been a colossal failure. It has failed in its essential function of educating the young. The best and the brightest emerge unscathed, but masses of students graduate semi-literate. A large fraction do not graduate from high school, dropping out frustrated and demoralized. In ghetto areas, the schools are arenas for crime and drug use. Politicians and educators spill millions of words about enforcing standards and holding school administrators responsible for the performance of their flocks. Nothing is likely to come of these initiatives, if only because the most important variable in student performance is the home atmosphere. The impoverished, single-parent, underclass environment is rarely the breeding ground of scholars. Meantime, the kids who cannot make it or don't try hold back the others. Everybody agrees that parochial and other private schools on average do a far better job of educating the young. As a product of the Jewish parochial schools of New York, I can vouch for the quality of the education. In New York there are hundreds of thousands of alumni like myself.

So my proposal is to get the government out of the education business. Abolish the public school system. Devolve the responsibility for educating children totally onto the parents. With a transition period, as I've said before. Students now in school could remain until they graduated—or dropped out. But there would be no new intake.

During the lengthy transition, private schools would expand—and new ones would come into existence, many lured by the prospect of profit—to accommodate the influx of new pupils. There are already many private firms in the education business in the United States. Many companies in other fields might find it attractive to set up technical schools to train a labor force that they could then hire. The variety of educational alternatives would expand, satisfying need and curiosity and appealing to individual desires and potential. I urge the curious to explore the DeVry Institute programs as examples of the private sector's response to this challenge.

One immediate objection is that poor parents could not afford the tuition. For one thing, there would be scholarships. Moreover, under my scheme of privatization—which goes beyond schools to other government activities—people of modest means would have more disposable income as the tax burden decreased dramatically. There would be no more school taxes, or a decline in property tax where separate school taxes are not levied, and no more federal aid to education. The relief to taxpayers would be greater than what parents would gain through the widespread availability of vouchers. I am not opposed to vouchers, but in my scheme of things vouchers would only be useful as an interim measure.

The same advantages of privatization apply to other government activities. Privatization fosters competition, if only in the form of competitive bidding when only one entity is required. Road repair is undertaken by private companies at the county level in many parts of the country. Why not in big cities as well, thereby eliminating the bureaucratic structures and high labor costs and waste of civil service departments? Restaurants and other businesses are normally compelled to hire private cartage companies to remove their garbage. Why not impose the same requirement on apartment houses and even on the ordinary householder? A practical way to do that would be competitive bidding for a cartage contract in each neighborhood or other subdivision of the city—one contract for each area.

Question 10.   What is your view of affirmative action?

Answer.   I am appalled at how the affirmative action program has developed. The whole thrust of the civil rights movement of the 1960s, in which I fervently believed (and still do), was to eradicate racial and ethnic discrimination in public facilities, housing and employment, and to make the ballot available to everyone. As a result of these initiatives, equality of opportunity would be promoted for all. But over the years the noble goal of equality of opportunity has been converted into equality of results. It has been a gradual and remorseless progression.

In the early 1960s, affirmative action meant "outreach" programs to get members of minority groups to apply for jobs from which they had previously been excluded and training programs to make them qualified. This was unexceptional—indeed a good idea. Then the federal government introduced the concepts of goals and timetables. Federal contractors—and most companies of any size had a federal contract of some sort—were compelled to establish realistic goals for the hiring and promotion of minority group members and timetables for the achievement of these goals. The government monitored companies' performance and cracked down on laggards. Before long, the goals became de facto quotas. Personnel departments found that if they met their numbers, they were off the hook. No matter if they shaved the qualifications a bit or if they thereby discriminated against majority group members. (The concept of reverse discrimination came into existence.) The goal—never averred, always denied—was thus equality of results, sometimes measured on the basis of the proportional representation of minorities. The same process went on in the field of higher education and in the allocation of government contracts on the local level. In the latter case, the program was often perverted by white firms getting minorities to front for them. It became a racket in some instances.

So I am appalled, to put it mildly. Defenders of the present system of affirmative action claim that it is essential because of the racial prejudice endemic in our society. They see preferential treatment— a term that they prefer not to use—as the only protection for the victims of discrimination. I find this absurd. There will always be prejudiced individuals, but the story of the last half century has been the economic emancipation and enfranchisement of millions of people. Affirmative action as now practiced is both unnecessary and invidious. It is also a good example of the unintended consequences of a well-intentioned government program. I still think it was proper for government to act—to demolish the edifice of segregation and discrimination, which violated every tenet of individual liberty. Now we need new laws, like the one in California, abolishing affirmative action.

Question 11.   As a libertarian, what do you think of the War on Drugs?

Answer.   I can respond as both a libertarian and an economist. The so-called War on Drugs can never be won. The basic reason is that the illegalization of the drug trade sets up perverse economic incentives. Because continual repression and the need to compensate criminals for the risk of serving time keep drug prices high, profits are huge and thus new entrants are continually enticed into the business to replace those packed off to jail. The prospect of high rewards makes people willing to assume high risks, just as in more respectable fields. At the retail end, the economic incentives spur pushers to recruit new users, especially among the young. Billions have been spent to outlaw the drug trade since the Harrison Act was passed in 1914 and the problem of drug abuse is far greater today than in that more innocent era. Massive amounts of drugs have been interdicted at the border, but more continues to flow in. Victories in the drug war involve variations in the use of drugs among different population groups. The numbers rise and fall. Treatment programs have their successes. But the problem remains, and nobody really thinks it is going to go away.

Decriminalization is the obvious solution. It would lower prices, make the drug trade far less attractive, and probably reduce gang wars in the ghetto. It would certainly depopulate the prisons. But drug use would probably increase for a time, despite the continuance of education programs and treatment programs. Alcoholism increased after prohibition ended in December 1933, but there is no discernible public interest in reinstalling it.

Question 12.   What would you do with the income tax? Would you replace it with the flat tax, favored by many conservatives?

Answer.   No. I would replace the income tax with a value-added tax (VAT). I agree that the flat tax is better than the current progressive income tax. Defenders of the present system argue that it is fairer than the flat tax because it imposes a larger burden as one moves up the income scale. So does the flat tax, but not to the same extent, which also means that the flat tax, like the present income tax, would provide a continual incentive to the rich to use every dodge, legal as well as illegal, to escape it.

By contrast, a value-added tax—a tax on consumption—could not be easily evaded. It is like a sales tax, but it is levied at every stage in the production of goods and services, with intermediate producers getting a rebate on the tax they paid and the ultimate consumer paying the final tax bill. The producers have no motive to evade the tax, for if they do not pass it on, they cannot collect the rebate. VAT has worked well in Europe. It would provide enough revenue in the United States, without any need for an income tax, whether flat or progressive, because of the reduction in government spending that I have advocated. The objection is often made that VAT would impose too heavy a burden on the poor, but that objection can be met by not taxing life's essentials like food, medicines, and rent below a specified level.

Appendix

Heresies That Have Stood the Test of Time

As the reader may have gathered, I've always taken some pleasure in being a bit ahead of the pack—not that I've advanced unconventional views simply for their shock value. I believed that I was correct in my diagnoses and prescriptions—and still do. Readers can, of course, judge that for themselves.

The first article in this Appendix, "Let's Abandon Earnings Per Share," printed on the editorial page of the *Wall Street Journal* on December 18, 1972, launched my columning career. That article was accompanied by the lead editorial the same day, which is also reproduced here. The other articles were based on newspaper columns that I contributed to the *Financial Times* of London and other papers. They are reprinted from the fourth edition (1980) of my book entitled *Analytical Methods in Financial Planning*, first published in 1974. By this time, much of the substance of these pieces has found its way into the corpus of conventional thinking, but these ideas were certainly heretical at the time, and they are still relevant.

Let's Abandon Earnings per Share

Joel Stern

The Associated Press recently added price/earnings ratios to the stock tables it distributes to newspapers, and a glance through the list shows that the P/E range on the New York Stock Exchange reaches from 2 to about 735. So if you know that a company's earnings per share are $1, you can have a high degree of confidence that the price of its stock will be between $2 a share and $735 a share.

Though even so cursory an examination might lead to the suspicion that there must be other important things, much of the financial and business world revolves around earnings per share, or EPS. Yet in fact determining the merit of corporate policies by their impact on per-share earnings is fraught with danger. EPS is too often a misleading indicator that can result in costly decisions that frequently shortchange the common shareholders.

The EPS criterion confuses investment decisions with financing policies. Substandard projects can appear desirable simply because of the way in which they are financed. Furthermore, a large body of empirical evidence indicates (as the range in P/E ratios suggests) that the market is not primarily interested in earnings or in EPS per se.

There are many reasons why management and the financial community should abandon EPS as an analytical tool. This is particularly true for acquisition pricing and financing and capital structure planning. Both executives and analysts need to take a closer look at the key elements that determine the price of a company's stock.

Acquisition Analysis

The rhetoric we read in many business publications about acquisition analysis is outrageous. Commonly, for instance, we are told that companies should make acquisitions because of the "earnings leverage" that will result.

171

As an example, let us assume that company A sells at a price/earnings multiple of 20 and that company B sells at a P/E of 10. Often, we are told that company A can offer B's shareholders a P/E of, say, 15—a premium of 50 percent—and that A can still increase its EPS. For each dollar of earnings A is buying, it only has to give up shares earning 75 cents. Thus, if A uses its shares to buy B and form a new company, AB, AB's EPS will always exceed A's EPS. Hence, we are told that the acquisition of B is good for A's shareholders. And, obviously, it is good for B's shareholders since they obtain a 50 percent premium above the market price of their shares.

But if we turn the example around, the danger in using EPS becomes obvious. If B buys A to form BA, B will pay at least A's P/E of 20. But now BA's EPS will be less than B's, because the company with the lower P/E must offer more shares per dollar of acquired earnings.

The same people who tell us that AB is good for A's shareholders tell us that BA is bad for B's shareholders, even though AB and BA are the same company, most often with the same assets and earnings expectations and, even, the same management. Should we expect AB and BA to sell at different prices in the market when they are really the same company?

A's acquisition of B or B's acquisition of A is in fact good for the buyer's shareholders only if synergism is expected. And the synergism must be at least large enough to justify the premium paid above the seller's current share price. Thus, it is illogical to claim that IBM, for example, can afford to pay more for B than could the Chase Manhattan Bank because IBM sells at a much higher P/E than Chase. If Chase can expect to generate larger synergism than IBM with the acquisition of B, shouldn't Chase be able to offer a greater price for B?

Furthermore, the business writer fails to realize that if IBM (or any firm selling at a high P/E) were to acquire firms for which it paid full value (i.e., there is no added benefit to the buyer's shareholders),

IBM's P/E would fall to offset the gain in EPS. Empirical evidence supports this position.

Confusing Investment with Financing

Another pitfall in using EPS as a guide for acquisition policy is confusing investment with financing. In one case the president of a well-diversified manufacturer selling at 16 times earnings wanted to acquire a small, but exceptionally profitable, engineering consulting firm for a P/E of 25. An equity swap would "dilute" the pro forma EPS. Facetiously, we suggested that he sell his company to the engineering firm, even though the latter was only about 10 percent as large as the manufacturer, so that the EPS would rise. He suggested an alternative: use debt to finance the acquisition. The anticipated profits from the acquisition would more than cover his company's out-of-pocket cost of interest on debt. Thus his company's income would rise while the number of outstanding shares would remain constant. He was right, the pro forma EPS would rise.

However, there is a conceptual problem with his suggestion. Since the pro forma EPS can be enhanced simply by employing debt, bad investments can appear to be good investments because the management can lever the firm and increase the EPS at the time the investment is undertaken. Furthermore, the management can increase the EPS without making any investment by borrowing to retire common shares. So there are many ways financing decisions can affect EPS, though they cannot change the intrinsic desirability of the acquisition, which is simply a multiplant decision. This means the investment decision must be made independently of the financing decision, or, in other words, on the basis of considerations other than the effect on EPS.

Thus, there are two distinct shortcomings to employing EPS as an analytical tool in acquisition pricing. First, the existing P/E's of the buyer and seller determine the decision, so that synergism may be excluded from consideration. Second, EPS can lead the decision-maker to believe that bad investments are good investment; simply lever the firm sufficiently at the time an investment is undertaken and EPS can be enhanced to any level desired by management.

The Benefits of Debt Financing

An emphasis on EPS not only misdirects management in selecting and pricing acquisitions, it also leads to ridiculous conclusions on the balance between debt and equity in a company's financial structure. Depending on the P/E multiple, mechanical dependence on EPS would lead to the expansion of debt to cover dubious projects, or to the elimination of all debt by issuing common shares. While in most cases an increase in the amount of debt in relation to equity will enhance EPS, in fact the benefits to a company's market value derived from its financing policies have nothing to do with EPS.

A company can use debt to increase its EPS so long as its after-tax return on fixed capital is larger than its after-tax interest costs. Today high-grade bonds cost the firm less than 4 percent after taxes. Thus, corporate investments in new plant and equipment yielding more than 4 percent after taxes would appear desirable to analysts emphasizing EPS. It is certainly not difficult to imagine the likely direction of IBM's share price if projects were undertaken earning a mere 5 percent on fixed capital, even if the EPS were rising.

The market will not ignore the fact that an increase in debt forces the common shareholder to assume greater financial risk, in the form of higher fixed costs due to interest expense. Without some factor to offset part of this new risk, the price/earnings multiple will decline. So the price of the common shares would remain unchanged despite the added EPS.

At the other extreme, the EPS criterion would dictate that high

P/E firms issue shares to retire debt. As it works out mathematically, EPS can be increased by issuing shares to retire debt so long as the price/earnings ratio is larger than the reciprocal of the after-tax borrowing rate. If a company's after-tax cost of borrowed funds is 4 percent, the reciprocal is one divided by 4 percent, or 25. Whenever the P/E exceeds 25, management can increase the EPS simply by issuing equity to retire debt. Hence, supporters of EPS maximization would recommend that companies selling at very high P/E's be debt free, a policy that would hardly be beneficial to the common shareholders.

There is considerable evidence that debt financing does add to the market value of a firm's common equity. Of course, the reason is that there is a factor that reduces part of the financial risk created by the fixed interest expense. The federal government bears a large portion of the financial risk—up to 48 percent, the corporate income tax rate. The deductibility of interest expense in calculating taxable income means that the company's earnings are reduced by up to only 52 percent of the cost of debt.

A large body of empirical evidence clarifies our intuition about borrowed capital, namely, that investors do not expect management to reduce debt. As it comes due, they expect management to refinance and, hence, maintain a particular target debt ratio. A target debt ratio implies that investors expect the annual tax saving to continue forever.

The present value of this perpetual stream is simply the corporate income tax rate multiplied by the amount of interest-bearing debt that is anticipated by the market. As long as the level of debt does not exceed prudent limits, the market value of firm's common shares will rise 48 cents for each dollar of interest-bearing debt in its target capital structure. Thus, the real benefit of debt financing to the common shareholders is not the added EPS; it is the government tax saving.

What Really Determines Prices?

It is clear that an EPS criterion frequently misallocates valuable corporate resources and shortchanges the shareholders. Nor, to judge by market behavior, is EPS the criterion that impresses investors, especially the sophisticated investors who really determine share prices. What do these investors look for in evaluating a company's overall performance?

Investors do not discount earnings per se. Consider two companies, X and Y. Assume that all we know is that their profits are expected to increase at identical annual rates of 15 percent. At this stage, a foolish question would be: which company should sell at a higher price, X or Y? Of course, the obvious answer is that we would expect X and Y to sell at an identical price, since, in the absence of additional information, X and Y are the same company!

However, with the addition of one other item about the two companies, we must conclude that X would command the greater market value: X requires almost no investment in new capital to increase its profits 15 percent annually, whereas Y requires a dollar of additional capital for each incremental dollar of sales. X sells at the higher price and price/earnings multiple because it requires less capital to grow at a given rate despite the fact that X and Y are expected to have identical future profits. That is, X has a larger expected rate of return on incremental capital. The key determinant of market value in this case is the expected return on incremental capital.

The implication we can draw from this example is that investors do not simply discount expected earnings; rather, investors discount anticipated earnings net of the amount of capital required to be invested in order to maintain an expected rate of growth in profits. This concept can be referred to as the expected future "Free Cash Flow." It is expected cash flow that is above and beyond the anticipated investment requirement of the business.

The key to successful acquisition analysis and capital structure planning is to focus on the determinants of market value that are employed by sophisticated investors. The pricing mechanism is to calculate the current value of the expected future free cash flow. The resulting EPS is unimportant.

Some Thinking to Do

Editorial in the *Wall Street Journal*

The article alongside by Joel Stern of Chase Bank is fascinating enough in its own right, but doubly intriguing in the context of the ongoing debate over the social responsibility of corporations. For in the end that debate comes down to the same question Mr. Stern discusses: How do you measure performance?

The official position of American business is that its job is to maximize profits. Businessmen may sometimes forget that this is not an end in itself but a means of discharging their social responsibility, but this is well understood by our best free-market philosophers. The objective of the profit-maximizing ethic, they remind us, is to promote efficient-use of resources, so that there will be a bigger pie to split among profits, wages and lower prices, to the total benefit of the entire community.

This is no frivolous position. The magnificent efficiencies of market economies remain under-appreciated; if the point is lost even on the Nixon administration and its wage-price controllers, a glance around the world shows that the free-market remains the engine of efficient production. Nor need the profit-maximizing position be any more self-serving than other conceptions of how to serve the public. Charges of business insensitivity, we've noticed, come easily from the lips of the well-educated class that now questions the need for greater material production—or, in other words, from $20,000-a-year people, quite willing to tell the average $10,000-a-year person he is too materialistic in wanting a higher standard of living.

Yet the profit-maximizing ethic does have its problems. Precisely what are "profits," for example, and over what time-frame are they to be maximized? We suppose the natural tendency of most corporations is to define "profits" as earnings-per-share [EPS], yet Mr. Stern surely demonstrates that the common emphasis on this criterion can lead to results that contribute neither to efficient use of resources nor to the total benefit of the community.

Surely no one could think that social benefits are achieved by a criterion that tells us that for company A to buy company B is good business but for company B to buy company A is bad business, though in fact AB and BA are the same company with the same prospects and the same contributions to make to the general welfare.

Thus many of the best free-market philosophers argue that a corporation should try to maximize not reported earnings but its share price, as a measure of its expected future economic contribution. Mr. Stern argues, for example, that the stock market in its wisdom sorts out the distortions of the EPS criterion, and that if a merger or particular financial structure does not contribute to economic efficiency neither will it contribute to a higher price for the company's stock.

Yet there is plenty of room to wonder whether the stock market really is as omniscient as this conception suggests. One does not need to rub shoulders along Wall Street very long to see stocks moved on the basis of "concepts" that have little if anything to do with economic efficiency. Perhaps these are merely the random errors of an ultimately efficient mechanism, but then again, perhaps not.

Do today's "sophisticated" investors really depend on keen appreciation of the underlying value that results from economic efficiency, or instead does their "sophistication" take the form of "recognizing" that it is all a psychological game, and that the trick is to spot the next fad a week earlier than the rest? The difference between an appreciation of true value and a bunch of dogs chasing each others' tails is no small one to the underlying philosophical justification for the stock market, and thus for the business world.

Beyond even that, the profit-maximizing ethic has to face up to situations in which all but the absolutely blind profit-maximizer would have the corporation settle for less than the maximum. Do we really want a corporation to squeeze the last bit of profit at the expense of making its employees acutely unhappy? Philosophers would square the circle by denying that this would ever maximize profits over the pertinent time-frame but this remains an unproved contention that does not resolve the philosophical difficulty. And if in some hypothetical situations we would have the managers do X, do we want an ethic that instructs them to do Y?

Now, none of this means that American business should forget about the profit criterion. So far the only alternative suggested under the rubric of social responsibility seems to be following the latest fad of our moralizing classes, which is to say, the fads of people foolish enough to think George McGovern a viable presidential candidate and to believe six other impossible things before breakfast.

At least the profit-maximizing ethic is plugged into reality somewhere, and in today's social milieu this is no small advantage. But the advantage often goes unappreciated because the profit-maximizing ethic is accepted on faith rather than understanding, and because its philosophical problems have gone unattended. If it is to protect its standing in the American community, American business has some thinking to do.

What if Capital Markets Are "Efficient"?

Several readers of this column have questioned my references to "sophisticated" investors and the implication that the stock market is efficient because such investors dominate it.

How, they ask, can you reconcile that view with the wild swing in prices we have seen in London and on Wall Street recently? How do you account for the fact that fads often account for price movements? Some of the critics appear to think that the market is dominated by unsophisticated investors who allegedly are looking for capital gains from price movements unrelated to anticipated future corporate profits.

To examine market behavior, one must define an "efficient" market and see what implications this holds for investment analysts and money managers.

A capital market allocates the ownership of an economy's capital. Ideally a market should provide a way for companies to raise money for profitable investment and for investors to purchase securities at prices which "fully reflect" all relevant information about companies' activities and prospects. In an efficient market, security prices always "fully reflect" available information.

In efficient capital markets, prices are "unbiased estimates" of "fair" market values. If the current price is not a "fair" one, it is just as likely to be above the fair price as below it. If investors believe that the market price and the fair price are different and, for this reason, buy shares, they will not in the long run make money. Occasionally, of course, they will make a profit; but over a period they will be incorrect often enough to cancel their gains.

In an efficient market, sophisticated investors ensure that fair prices and market prices are almost always the same. Sophisticated investors make strenuous efforts to lay their hands on price-sensitive information so that they can identify overvalued and undervalued securities before anyone else.

However, in reality, sophisticated investors rarely outperform the market, which shows that, individually, they have no monopoly of price-sensitive information. If they did have a monopoly, other investors would no longer attempt to seek new information and the market, starved of well-briefed operators, would become inefficient.

An important concomitant is that in efficient markets, unsophisticated investors are protected by the activities of their sophisticated brethren. In other words, even if some investors do not understand the securities markets, their sales and purchases on average and over time will be at fair prices.

Thus, the market performance of sophisticated and unsophisticated investors should be about the same. The unsophisticates could, however, do worse if they make an excessive number of buy-sell transactions and incur heavy costs.

In efficient markets, investors can achieve a performance equal to the market as a whole simply by selecting securities at random. This means that security analysis is a waste of time once efficiency has been established unless analysts' recommendations consistently outperform market indices. Even if a particular analyst does outfox the other foxes, his performance may only be equal to the market as a whole if his recommendations are adjusted for risk.

For example, assume the stock market rises 10 percent in value through cash dividends and price appreciation. If an analyst's recommendations are twice as risky as the general market, he must earn 20 percent in nominal terms to equal the market's performance in real terms. Only if he earns above 20 percent has he outperformed the market. If superior performance cannot be achieved, the only sensible portfolio strategy is a randomly selected buy-and-hold policy.

If investors wish to take more or less risk than the market, risk should be calculated for various alternative portfolios. Then the investor's risk preferences should be matched with randomly selected portfolios of identical risk. Identifying investor's risk preferences and selecting suitable portfolios is the investment advisor's role in efficient markets. These days it is perfectly possible to measure investment risk.

Although risk-adjusted rates of return are the correct way of measuring performance, they are not widely used among the financial community. When the performance of security analysts and money managers is measured on a risk-adjusted basis, the evidence shows that the "experts" do not outperform the market.

Fewer Analysts, Please: Why People Believe Capital Markets Are "Inefficient"!

The world's capital markets need well-informed professional investors to make them efficient. Over the past decade much evidence has been accumulated to show that capital markets in general, and stock markets in particular, are indeed efficient.

One can call a capital market efficient if (1) security prices always "fully reflect" available information determining a company's intrinsic, or fair, market value, and (2) no investors in the market have a monopoly of price-sensitive information.

Since a company's current share price is based on current information about expected risk and profitability, the first condition implies that predicting future share prices requires investors to forecast tomorrow's information about changes in risk and profitability. The second condition implies that few analysts or investors can predict tomorrow's information accurately and consistently enough to outperform the market.

The two conditions together imply that investors who employ trading rules to select investments based on available information cannot outperform a simple buy-and-hold policy. It is not difficult to see why many analysts and investors believe that efficient markets do not—or had better not—exist.

Reasons

Three main reasons can be advanced for their skepticism: (1) Imperfections in the real world destroy the efficiency with which prices adjust to new information; or (2) prices change for no apparent economically justifiable reason; or (3) vested interests misinterpret or disregard evidence which shows that capital markets are efficient.

Although each view has many supporters, only the first is intellectually honest. A capital market is perfectly efficient if three

184

conditions are met so that prices can adjust quickly to new information. First, investors incur no transaction costs when buying or selling securities. Second, relevant information is freely available to all security analysts and investors without charge. Third, all analysts and investors agree on the likely impact of available information on current and future prices. In the real world, none of these conditions applies and so perfect market efficiency is unattainable.

Even without these conditions being met, however, capital markets are sufficiently efficient provided (1) investors take account of all relevant information in determining prices, including transaction costs; (2) enough major investors have access to all relevant information; (3) these investors cannot consistently outperform the market using available information.

Transactions costs, poor communication of information and disagreement about its significance all reduce market efficiency. However, only empirical study can show whether these factors are sufficiently important to reject the market efficiency view. The main body of evidence points to a high degree of efficiency in several of the world's major capital markets.

Financial "experts" are wrong when they say that individual market prices (or a price index) change for no economically justifiable reason. Their preoccupation with the immediate cause of a price change shows that they do not realize that market prices are determined by expectations about the future. Ironically, they compound their error by failing to identify the market's earlier expectation when it is confirmed by information published in the press.

Almost daily we read about a sudden rise or fall in a company's share price. Since the cause of the change is frequently unclear, investment analysts often ask the company to comment. When the company replies that it too is surprised about the price behavior, the analyst often comments: "Once again, the market is behaving 'foolishly,' or 'irrationally,' or, as I would say, 'inefficiently.'" Since share prices are based on what people believe will happen tomorrow, justifiable reasons for yesterday's market behavior, which were not apparent earlier, are forthcoming today and are too easily overlooked (a sudden change in a company's order book backlog, sales or earnings).

Price Changes

One can only sympathize with the broker who announces daily why market prices rose or fell, perhaps, by half a percent. It is even a little amusing when he employs the same reason for explaining price increases *and* price declines. It is remarkable that "expert" opinions continue to be publicized!

Empirical evidence shows that there are more security analysts employed than are needed to maintain market efficiency. Not surprisingly, the analysts themselves tend to disregard such uncomfortable evidence. However, when the investment bankers and brokers provide financial support for research on the efficiency of capital markets and then fail to report the results to their customers, one can reach only two possible conclusions: either the merchant bankers and brokers do not understand the empirical work, a doubtful assumption in view of their commitment to the research; or they have conveniently and understandably disregarded it.

Forthcoming columns will be devoted to presenting and explaining this empirical work so that readers can reach their own conclusions.

Are "Technicians" an Endangered Species?

"Technicians" are security analysts who employ trading rules to generate superior investment performance. Their large arsenal of tools includes: charts of historical prices for detecting patterns that are allegedly useful in forecasting future prices; filter systems, in which buy and sell signals supposedly result from arbitrary percentage price increases or decreases, respectively; and, price-volume systems in which future prices are apparently detected from changes in the volume of shares traded.

Each of these technical tools, and many others, have considerable intuitive appeal and enjoy great popularity among brokers and institutional investors. However, tests of these tools conclude that trading rules are unable to outperform a simple buy-and-hold investment strategy.

Requisites for Rules

Trading rules can provide superior investment performance only if sequences of prices conform to discernible and predictable patterns. That is, more than intuition is needed to produce superior results; successive price changes must not be independent. Only then can technicians hope to survive by providing an economically useful service.

To date, there is virtually no evidence in support of technicians' claims, whereas there is overwhelming evidence that trading rules are useless.

Nature of Evidence

The evidence that disclaims technical analysis results from studies which prove that capital markets are dominated by financially sophisticated investors who quickly evaluate new information about companies' risks and expected profitability and impound this information into market prices. The result is that market prices and intrinsic (i.e., fair) prices are almost always identical.

When security prices fully reflect all available relevant information about risks and expected profitability and no investor (or group of investors) possesses monopoly control of this information, the capital market is called "efficient."

If today's security prices reflect all currently available relevant information, future prices become solely a function of new information that will be available tomorrow. Even if historical prices are important to investors, this information is public knowledge today and, hence, it can only affect market prices investors agree are fair today. However, a very great degree of market efficiency must be proven before we can reject the possibility of the potential benefits of technical trading rules.

Before the body of evidence is examined, it would be helpful to identify the degree of market efficiency that is essential to disprove the value of trading rules.

Three Forms of Efficiency

The degree of market efficiency often is described in three distinct forms: the weak form, the semi-strong form, and the strong form.

In its weak form, market efficiency means that current prices fully reflect information derived from historical sequences of prices. It implies that possessing knowledge about historical sequences of prices does not aid investors in selecting securities.

The semi-strong form states that public information about specific companies' financial data is fully reflected in the firms' current share prices and, hence, obtaining and analyzing this information cannot result in superior investment performance.

The strong form asserts that even if investors possess privileged information, they cannot benefit from it, because enough sophisticated investors pursue this kind of information and impound it into share prices.

A recommendation for abandoning technical analysis only requires evidence in support of the weak form that knowledge about sequences of historical prices does not enhance investment results, which implies that price patterns do not exist, i.e., successive price changes are random, or unpredictable.

(Future columns will present evidence in support of the semi-strong and strong forms of market efficiency.)

Early Evidence

The earliest evidence regarding the absence of price patterns dates back to 1900. In that year, a study by Louis Bachelier (whose paper is reproduced in Professor Paul Cootner's book, *The Random Character of Stock Market Prices* [Cambridge, Mass.: MIT, 1964]), found an absence of price patterns in France's commodities markets.

In 1953, Maurice Kendall reported corroborating evidence in British share prices and in New York commodities markets for cotton and wheat (see: *The Journal of the Royal Statistical Society*, 161.96, Part I 1953, pp. 11–25). He found that weekly price changes were completely unpredictable, i.e., random.

Harry Roberts, in 1959, demonstrated that numbers selected randomly had the same appearance as a time series of share prices on the New York Stock Exchange (see: *Journal of Finance*, March, 1959, pp. 1–10). Ironically, both Roberts' selected series of share prices and his randomly selected number series were remarkably similar to so-called "head-and-shoulder patterns" so popular with technicians for forecasting share prices.

Also in 1959, M. F. M. Osborne, a distinguished physicist with the Naval Research Laboratory in Washington, D.C., reported that share price movements on the New York Stock Exchange and the motion of physical objects, i.e., "Brownian motion," were very similar. The latter are completely unpredictable (see: *Operations Research*, March-April, 1959, pp. 145–173).

Tests during 1960s

The development of a framework for price formation (i.e., various degrees of market efficiency) originated with professors Paul Samuelson in 1965 (see: *Industrial Management Review*, Spring, 1965, pp. 41–49) and Benoit Mandelbrot in 1966 (see: *Journal of Business*, Special Supplement, January, 1966, pp. 242–255).

As a result of their path-breaking efforts, more extensive tests were conducted during the 1960s by Arnold B. Moore in 1962 (see: Paul Cootner's book, pp. 139–161) and Eugene Fama in 1965 (see: *Journal of Business*, January, 1965, pp. 34–105). These tests covered longer periods of time and involved more complex statistical procedures that were designed to avoid spurious results.

Moore examined weekly changes of 29 randomly selected common shares on the New York Stock Exchange for the years 1951–1958. He found that weekly price changes were useless in predicting future price changes.

Fama investigated successive price changes, lagged price changes for periods of one, four, nine, and sixteen days and directional price changes (i.e., increases vs. decreases in prices) of the 30 shares in the New York market's Dow Jones Industrial Average for the period 1957–1962.

Although Moore found virtually no discernible price patterns, Fama detected a very slight pattern. However, minimal transactions costs incurred even by floor traders who own Exchange seats eliminated the possibility of profiting from trading rules.

Technicians frequently argued that these tests excluded more complicated price patterns. Thus, in 1961 and 1964, Sidney Alexander attempted to design a successful filter system in which purchases and sales were made automatically after arbitrary percentage price increases and decreases, respectively (see: *Industrial Management Review*, May, 1961, pp. 7–26, and Spring, 1964, pp. 25–46). Although his results refuted the weak form of market efficiency because he detected price patterns, Fama in 1965 and Fama and Marshall Blume in 1966 (see: *Journal of Business Security Prices: A Supplement*, January, 1966, pp. 226–241) corrected Alexander's errors and found that the patterns disappeared. Alexander, first, had failed to include transactions costs and, second, he had assumed that shares could be bought or sold at the price at which the buy or sell signal was made.

Unfortunately, space limitations prevent an examination of many other studies conducted by Michael Jensen, Robert Levy, George Parker, Clive Granger and Oskar Morgenstern, all of which support the existence of the weak form of market efficiency.

Conclusions

In view of this bountiful evidence, the inescapable conclusions are that:

1. Technical analysis may be fun, but it is not profitable for investors. It is virtually useless for improving investment performance. Trading rules do not outperform a simple buy-and-hold portfolio strategy.
2. Transaction costs that result from trading can ultimately bankrupt investors who rely solely on technical analysis.
3. Since considerable support for the weak form of market efficiency dates back more than 20 years, financial sophistication apparently was present in the market before institutional investors entered it in a major way in recent years.

Are "Fundamental" Security Analysts Necessary?

Most "popular" books about the functioning of capital markets contain one or two extreme themes: either investors can make enormous profits by employing a few simple rules, or they haven't a chance of generating even meager returns because markets are dominated by insiders or large financial institutions.

Although these intuitive themes can provide comfort to investors who have experienced poor investment results, a large body of evidence indicates that several capital markets are dominated by financially sophisticated investors and that their actions serve to maintain a close relationship between market prices and intrinsic (i.e., fair) values. The fact that these markets function "efficiently" has considerable implications for security analysts, money managers, and corporate management. However, the significance of these implications is limited by the degree of market efficiency.

Weak Form

The least efficient market is often described as the "weak form," which means that current prices fully reflect information derived from historical sequences of prices. This form of market efficiency implies that knowledge about historical sequences of prices does not aid investors in selecting securities. That is, even if patterns or trends in historical prices can be detected, they are not useful in predicting future prices. Consequently, in markets that demonstrate at least the weak form of efficiency, technical analysis (e.g., charting and other trading rules) is a useless device for generating superior investment performance.

Our last column presented considerable published evidence in support of the existence of the weak form of efficiency.

Semi-Strong Form

A slightly greater degree of market efficiency is often referred to as the "semi-strong form," in which public information about specific companies' financial data is fully reflected in the firms' current share prices. The implication is that obtaining and analyzing this information cannot result in superior investment performance.

If this form of efficiency can be proven, the activities of many security analysts who attempt to identify undervalued or overvalued shares by studying financial data (i.e., "fundamentalists") may be superfluous. That is, a minimum number of fundamental analysts are needed to assure efficiency; but once efficiency is attained, additional analysis is fruitless.

The purpose of this column is to present evidence in support of the semi-strong form. Our next column will examine evidence regarding the greatest degree of market efficiency, the "strong form," which states that possessing privileged information does not benefit investors.

Evidence

Because the semi-strong form of market efficiency is concerned with the extent to which prices fully reflect public knowledge about firms' prospects, empirical studies have focused on the speed with which new information is impounded into share prices.

Three extensive studies indicate that market prices adjust very quickly to the release of public information, which bears on a firm's expected risks and profitability.

The procedure followed in these studies was, first, to determine the relationship between the actual rates of return on individual shares through cash dividends and capital appreciation and the rates of return on the market as a whole. Second, the impact of the specific issue under study on this relationship was examined. If the relationship was not altered, except to the extent that the issue under study altered expectations about the rates of return on the shares of the companies affected, the market was judged to have conformed to the semi-strong form of efficiency.

1. *Earnings Announcements*

Ray Ball and Philip Brown examined the extent to which the market anticipates announcements of earnings increases and decreases by corporate management (see: *Journal of Accounting Research*, Autumn, 1968, pp. 159–178).

To detect the effect of earnings announcements, Ball and Brown studied deviations from the relationship between rates of return on individual shares and the market as a whole for 261 companies for the period 1946–1966. These companies were divided into two groups, one for companies whose earnings rose relative to the market and one for companies whose earnings declined relative to the market. They found that for both groups of companies, the earnings announcements were anticipated by the market. That is, share prices adjusted to the new information well in advance of management's announcements. In many instances, the period of anticipation was almost twelve months. This is strong support for market efficiency.

2. *Stock Splits*

Eugene Fama, Lawrence Fisher, Michael Jensen, and Richard Roll evaluated the significance of stock splits in communicating corporate managements' expectations about profit prospects. Their hypothesis was that stock splits convey information to the market about dividend increases which, in turn, communicate managements' confidence about future earnings (see: *International Economic Review*, February, 1969, pp. 1–21). In a market displaying semi-strong efficiency, splits affect share prices only to the extent that investors' earnings expectations are altered and are quickly reflected by changes in share prices.

Fama, Fisher, Jensen, and Roll examined all stock splits of at least 25 percent on the New York Stock Exchange from 1927 through 1959. There were 940 splits for 622 different securities. They found that share prices did not rise or fall more than would have been expected after abstracting general movements in the market as a whole during the months surrounding the time of the stock split. The share prices of companies that split rose dramatically, relative to the market as a whole, well in advance of the announcement of the split when dividend increases followed the split within a year. A likely explanation for this share price behavior is that splits occur after the market becomes aware of improved profit prospects. Hence, this study provides considerable support for the semi-strong form of market efficiency.

3. *Secondary Offering*

Myron Scholes studied the informational content of large secondary offerings (see: *Journal of Business*, April, 1972, pp. 179–211).

Scholes examined the price effects of secondary offerings in order to separate the effects of the distribution (i.e., selling pressure) from the information inherent in the distribution about profit prospects. On average, he found that at the time of the distribution the share price declined by less than 2 percent. Because there was no relationship between the size of the distribution and the size of the price decline, he concluded that the decline was caused by the information content of managements' actions. Thus, the largest declines accompanied sales by corporate officers and the company itself, and the impact of the secondary was fully reflected within six days. Since the Securities and Exchange Commission does not require identification of the seller until six days after the distribution, Scholes concluded that the market fully anticipated the information contained in the offering. He found identical results in the new issue market, too. Hence, Scholes's work is further support of the semi-strong form of market efficiency.

The conclusions are inescapable. Based on considerable evidence:

1. Market prices adjust extremely fast to new relevant information.
2. It is almost certainly fruitless to analyze information about companies that is readily available to the public in the hope that undervalued or overvalued securities can be identified.
3. The number of analysts engaged in fundamental security analysis may be far in excess of the number required to maintain an efficient market.

Companies Should Avoid Sharp Swings in Dividends

Too often, boards of directors establish or alter dividend policies for the wrong reasons. They attempt to communicate management's expectations about profitability by changing the dividend payout substantially, or, worse, they subordinate the firm's dividend policy to their investment decision-making. In both cases, the unfortunate and unintended by-products often are a considerable decline in their shareholders' wealth and a greater volatility of share price movements.

These results, however, are unnecessary. Formulating a proper role for the firm's dividend policy could enhance the shareholders' wealth and generate more confidence in the company's management. A recent example is representative and illustrates the problem. (All data have been disguised.)

Dividend as a Communication Device

Not long ago, a manufacturer asked us to evaluate a proposal to increase the cash dividend paid to its common shareholders. In the late 1950s, the company had paid 50 cents a share annually. Shortly thereafter, its profitability deteriorated, and, hence, the board of directors voted to reduce the dividends to 20 cents, about 50 percent of management's estimate of "normalized" profits (i.e., profits adjusted for unusual and non-recurring events).

But now that the company's performance had improved substantially—profits were up 180 percent over the past five years to $1.30 a share in 1972—the senior financial officer (SFO) suggested that the cash dividends be increased to 50 cents. His objective was to demonstrate the permanence or recurring nature of the company's profitability. If the company's dividend payments were raised substantially, the SFO believed the market would interpret the change in policy as management's conviction that recent profit levels were here to stay. The view was that management would hardly increase the dividend payment to a level it could not expect to service.

This appeared to be a reasonable presumption. However, we were told that the company anticipated substantial needs for capital on which it expected to earn a much greater rate of return than its shareholders could hope to earn by investing in other securities of similar risk. The natural question to ask was: why pay out profits with one hand that the company will have to ask the shareholders to return to the other hand, especially if management expects to do better with funds retained in the business?

The Best Dividend Policy

If in the real world there were no income taxes and no costs of buying or selling securities, the proper dividend policy would be to pay out nothing to the shareholders, if management expected to earn more on new investments than the shareholders would expect by investing elsewhere in securities of similar risk. In this hypothetical world, investors could sell shares occasionally to obtain cash for their immediate subsistence or to invest elsewhere in real estate, savings accounts, etc.

In the real world of both taxes and transactions costs, a large number of investors prefer cash dividends because they pay little or no taxes on ordinary income. Included in this group are many retired people and large pension funds. For others in high income tax brackets, little or no cash dividends are preferable because the costs of capital gains taxes and selling securities are far less than the tax on ordinary income. Hence, an interesting phenomenon occurs when a company sells shares to the public for the first time. A clientele effect builds up as investors with particular needs are attracted to the company for, among other reasons, the tax consequences of the dividend policy.

Therefore, if management's objective is to act in the best interests of its company's shareholders, it should never alter the fraction of normalized earnings to be paid out as cash dividends. The dividend payout ratio (i.e., dividends paid as a percent of earnings) should be maintained in order that the return expected by the shareholders from dividends remains a fixed percent of the total return they expect on the average over a period of time from dividends plus capital appreciation. This will occur as long as the average price/earnings ratio does not change significantly over time.

This policy should be maintained during exceptional and poor years. If a substantial decline in profits was reported in 1972 but management foresaw bright prospects for 1973, any decline in the dividend payment in 1972 should have been based on their [management's] judgment of the permanent nature of the earnings drop. Likewise, an increase in profits that resulted from a decline in interest rates (e.g., the business of a bond dealer) should have been considered non-recurring, unless management expected interest rates to continue falling in 1971 and beyond.

Returning to the case of the manufacturer, the board of directors had a conscious policy of paying out about 50 cents of dividends for each dollar of normalized earnings. When the company's earnings declined in the late 1950s, the policy should have been maintained. However, the board of directors of the company reduced the fraction of earnings paid out as dividends during the 1960s, principally because the earnings grew rapidly and the dividend payments remained 20 cents a share annually.

Ten years is far too long for the shareholders to delay altering their investment portfolios in order to obtain their accustomed, expected and desired payout. The shareholders would have increased their investment in other higher dividend–paying shares in order to realize their desired level of current ordinary income. Thus, the best policy for the manufacturer today would be to increase the dividend payment at the same rate as the rate of growth in normalized earnings, maintaining the lower payout ratio of the last few years, because the shareholders today would want this policy. It would afford them the greatest after-tax return on their investment.

Subordinating Dividends to Investment Policy

Many companies that have large capital needs exceeding their internally generated cash flow reduce their dividend payout ratios *because* their managements expect greater rates of return on new investments than the shareholders could expect to earn by investing in other securities of similar risk. The management's rationale is that such a policy is in their shareholders' best interest. It is true that investment opportunities that are expected to outperform the shareholders' options should increase the price of the company's common shares. But it is necessary to separate investment policy from financing policy. Management should evaluate its uses of funds independent of its sources of funds. Thus, profitable investments for the shareholders should be undertaken, but dividend policy need not (and should not!) be altered in order to accommodate the investment strategy.

Aside from the cost and tax trade-offs mentioned earlier, retaining earnings (rather than paying out dividends) is equivalent to paying dividends *and* issuing new shares of common equity to replace the dividend payment. That is, dividend policy is a financing decision that should be considered by management to be independent of the firm's investment policy. If superior investment opportunities are available to the firm, the shareholders want them to be undertaken by issuing new common shares (if necessary) rather than [by] cutting back on cash dividends.

Once again, our decision rule is that dividend policy should be stable in relation to normalized earnings because the clientele of shareholders wants the greatest, consistent after-tax rate of return on their investment. Subordinating dividend policy to investment policy confuses investment decisions with the firm's financing policy.

Why Dividends Do Not Matter

We all know that increases in cash dividends paid to ordinary shareholders have traditionally been associated with increases in share price. This dividend-price (DP) relationship is usually expressed as cause-and-effect. In other words, a company can influence its share price by changing its dividend policy. An increase in the proportion of profits paid out in dividends is assumed to increase the company's share price. The reverse is also said to be true.

This DP relationship, if valid, has important implications for corporate management and for governments. Because the DP relationship infers that investors prefer a dollar of dividends to a dollar of share price appreciation, managements are led to believe that they will maximize their shareholders' total return (in dividends and capital appreciation) only if they pay generous cash dividends.

If the government attempts a wage-and-price-control policy, the DP relationship will lead to a reduction in the proportion of profits paid out in dividends. The U.K. and U.S. governments' policies of restricting dividend increases suggests that government officials must believe in the DP relationship. My experience with senior management is that they, too, are proponents of the DP relationship.

There is, however, an alternative view which is not only intuitively more appealing but is also backed by strong evidence showing that the DP relationship is a myth. Its proponents believe that although tax is levied at a higher rate on cash dividends than on capital gains, one form of return to shareholders is not more desirable than the other. Consequently, managements and governments should abandon policies which attach any significance to the role of dividends in determining share prices—because dividends do not matter.

Until 1961, traditionalists believed that dividend policy directly affected share prices. Then Merton H. Miller and Franco Modigliani (MM) presented a theoretical basis for rejecting the DP relationship. They said that if a company did not permit its dividend policy to affect its investment decisions, and if taxes and the costs of buying and selling shares were ignored, dividend policy should have no impact on share prices. MM showed that earnings retained to finance corporate growth were equivalent to a compulsory rights issue because (disregarding investors' needs for current consumption) dividends not paid to the shareholders, in effect, would be reinvested in the company's common shares.

However, MM suggested that the broker commissions and the different tax rates on income and capital gains could alter investors' indifference to dividend policy. Low-income investors would be attracted to shares paying large cash dividends, whereas high-income investors would not want such dividends. That is, corporate dividend policies would attract a specific clientele of investors. MM hinted that, despite this clientele effect, dividend policy might not alter share prices, if a management sets a dividend policy to meet the collective needs of all investors who want a particular payout level. Once the demand-supply forces were met, changes in dividend policy would result in changes in clientele, but not in share prices. If share prices could be altered by changes in the proportion of profits paid out in dividends, managements would do so until the demand for specific dividend policies was saturated, thereby eliminating the impact of dividend policy on share prices.

This view of stock market behavior rejects not only the DP relationship, but also the idea that institutional factors (differential taxes, transaction costs) and the resulting clientele effect make dividend policy affect share prices.

Fischer Black and Myron Scholes have advanced this theory one more critical step in a penetrating article, "The Effects of Dividend Yield and Dividend Policy on Common Stock Prices and Returns," in the *Journal of Financial Economics* (May, 1974).

Black and Scholes (B&S) add another reason for investor indifference to dividend payout. They show that companies with high dividend yields have unique risk characteristics that differ significantly from low-dividend-yield companies. Consequently, investors who concentrate their portfolios in one type of dividend yield will hold shares that are not as well diversified as portfolios comprising a combination of high and low yielding shares.

B&S are surprised at the preponderance of companies which pay generous dividends, since intuitively it seems that the demands of investors who prefer capital gains to dividends for tax reasons are not satisfied.

Not only do B&S provide a theory for this observation. They also present evidence that dividends do not matter, even when investors' tax preferences are taken into account. They show that "it is not possible to demonstrate . . . that the returns on high yield securities are different from the returns on low yield securities either before or after taxes." To account for this startling discovery, they claim that because an investor has no way of knowing how to alter his portfolio's dividend yield to increase its expected return, and because of the lost diversification of doing so, he probably decides to ignore dividend yield entirely.

The conclusions are that managements can ignore the consequences of changing their dividend policy on its share price, because there are none; and that governments which limit dividends as part of a wage-and-price-control policy will not accomplish their objective.

Risk Matters

Every investor knows that different shares carry different risk—even if, at the present time, they all seem too risky. It is perhaps less widely recognized that the degree of risk can be measured. Furthermore, many managers do not realize that this relationship between risk and share price can have a bearing on their own business decisions.

Take financing policy and investment decisions, for instance. Different policies will make the company's shares more or less risky investments. A management which understands risk can calculate the impact of its financing and investment decisions on the share price before they are actually implemented.

To understand risk, one may start with the stock market. Suppose the stock market rises on average by 10 percent over a period and that a particular portfolio's value goes up by 20 percent. The temptation is to conclude that the portfolio performance is twice as good as the market average. This would be misleading, however, because it leaves out all consideration of risk. For instance, if the portfolio is twice as risky as the market, the true risk-adjusted performance is no better than average.

Security analysts, portfolio managers and even the general run of investors need to be able to measure this risk in order to make a realistic assessment of the performance of an investment portfolio. But from the point of view of management, the important thing to establish is whether there is a link between equity risk, on the one hand, and a company's intrinsic (or fair) share value and its cost of equity capital.

Equity risk can be measured by the likelihood that a shareholder will be able to sell his common shares tomorrow at today's price. If a firm's share price is expected to fluctuate very little, the shareholders' risk is small. The converse is also true.

Studies of share price movements show that historical rates of share price volatility usually continue for long periods. This means that investors really can get an accurate measure of the risk they are taking by studying the historical share price patterns.

For instance, the risk in the common shares of public utilities, which fluctuate very little, is small. In contrast, because machine tool and industrial machinery share prices are very volatile, their shareholders' equity risk is relatively large.

Risk is generally measured in terms of expected variability. The less predictable an expected return, the greater is its riskiness. Intrinsic share values are obtained by discounting a firm's expected future Free Cash Flow at its cost of capital. Free Cash Flow—FCF—is equal to net operating profit after taxes—NOPAT—minus the amount of new capital investment needed to generate future NOPAT. FCF is the expected return.

(This cost of equity capital is the minimum rate of return that management must earn on new projects to compensate shareholders for the business and financial risk they are running. [Management] should be able to offer at least as high a return as could be obtained by investing in alternative, equally risky portfolios.)

A firm's cost of capital is directly related to the risk investors perceive in expected future FCF being realized in practice. The greater the variability in future FCF, the greater is the risk and, hence, the cost of capital. And the greater is the cost of capital (the discount rate for FCF), the smaller is the intrinsic share value.

The relationship between share price volatility and the firm's cost of capital can be illustrated by a simple example. Assume that the relationship between a firm's share price and its current and expected FCF is constant over time. Fluctuations in the share price represent fluctuations in the market's estimate of the firm's expected future FCF. Share price volatility is a measure of the expected variability in future FCF and, hence, the cost of capital.

In conclusion, three important statements can be made about share price volatility:

1. Price volatility is a measure of investors' equity risk: it is the mechanism by which the market communicates its expectations about risk to corporate management.
2. Investors' equity risk is closely related to the market's perception of the anticipated variability in a company's future FCF.
3. Because anticipated variability in future FCF determines the magnitude of a firm's cost of capital, share price volatility and cost of capital are directly related.

Acknowledgments

I wish to express gratitude to people who inspired me on a personal level and who stimulated my intellectual curiosity, which led me to the frontiers of thinking in financial microeconomics. My parents, Boris and Irene Stern, now of blessed memory, inspired their children to reach within themselves, even under the most difficult circumstances, while maintaining a humanity and empathy for others who were less fortunate while providing warmth and caring within our family—and this extended to aunts, uncles, and cousins. There was only one way to behave, and that was with the utmost integrity, as if the Almighty was witnessing every thought and action. Charity was a daily essential, but anonymously, so that we would not know who received it and the recipient would not know who gave it.

Nobody could have known, especially me, what studying at the University of Chicago would mean for my professional development. As a youngster, I had never heard of Milton Friedman, Merton Miller, and George Stigler, later to become Nobel laureates. The most important thing these three towers of intellectual curiosity did was to help me understand and obtain a grasp for the functioning of markets. Their teaching and class atmosphere helped me see the intuitive correctness of this point of view. Either people believe in markets as a basis for the allocation of resources and in individual liberty as the fundamental human right, or they don't. In Professor Friedman's class, he defined the difference between arrogance and humility. Humility was the belief that we could be wrong in our point of view if through voluntary discussion we failed to convince others. In contrast, arrogance meant that we would use coercion to make certain that our opponent adopted our point of view. So simple and so clear. Professor George Stigler helped us understand the institutional issues regarding regulation and government intervention in general, but Merton Miller possessed one other quality. He wanted us to be friends, and that we were. My comments and questions in class often frustrated him because I had no background in economics before arriving in Chicago; and yet he would take the time to make sure I understood the propositions that were critical and the sequence of timing that was necessary in understanding problems and their solutions.

On a personal level, John Shiely, with whom I wrote the book *The EVA Challenge*, published in 2001, has been the prime example of how a business friendship blossoms into warmth and caring that is so essential as we pass through life. Here is a man who is the chief executive of Briggs & Stratton in Milwaukee and finds the time to be a brilliant musician and bandleader, winning trophies along the way. For years, I have joined him and his family at the annual concert in Milwaukee, inspiring me to not forget that there is so much more in life than just one's vocation.

The most difficult recognition is the one that involves recognizing one's personal failure. Quick to success, with successes followed by even greater success, can lead one down the wrong path to an invariable arrogance, and that was my locus by the mid-1970s. Irving ("Yitz") Greenberg, Rav Avi Weiss, and J. Geldzahler are amongst the greatest human beings, as well as spiritual leaders, whom I have ever encountered, balancing family and community concerns with pastoral inspiration, but never condescending to another human being, and I mean never, never. During one religious service, conducted by

ACKNOWLEDGMENTS

"Yitz," decorum had broken down and one could barely hear the service. When he stepped to the podium and looked out over the congregation, all of us expected him to give the congregation a tongue-lashing. Instead, he asked how we could make life easier for the congregants who wanted to be inspired by the religious service. He suggested that the congregants listen carefully and that alone would provide the inspiration. What a magnificent demonstration!

There are the important day-to-day contributions made to my life by the support and stimulation provided by the staff at Stern Stewart & Co. When we jumped ship from the Chase Manhattan Bank in 1982, our paths could have led to failure, but the commitment, the focus, and the devotion of our people to our objective and to each other has been a great source of menschligkeit to me. Three of our founding partners—Donald Chew, David Glassman, and Bennett Stewart—remain with me from that original cast; and there are so many other people who have been critical in establishing our reputation that I fear omitting one by mentioning others. They are my colleagues and they are my friends at the same time.

My glorious friendship with Brian and Shirley Kantor of Cape Town was one of the most important reasons that I accepted an invitation to be a visiting professor at the University of Cape Town for six weeks a year for five years and to build a house near theirs in the most lovely of communities, Camps Bay, a suburb just three miles from the heart of Cape Town.

Finally, I am greatly indebted to my sisters, Roberta and Jackie, their husbands, Bernie and Barry, and their lovely children. Nothing draws me closer to home than the love I feel when next we are to share the blessings of family.

JOEL M. STERN

Index